PRAISE FOR *WISE CONFIDENCE*

"*Wise Confidence* masterfully presents a road map to self-empowerment, illuminating the journey from self-doubt to authenticity. The book's unique blend of psychology, spirituality, and personal growth creates a comprehensive guide for building lasting self-assurance. As someone who writes and teaches about trauma, I'm often looking for resources to recommend, and this is one. If you're seeking a transformative shift from limitation to empowerment, Dienstmann is a powerful guide to uncovering your true potential."

DAVID A. TRELEAVEN, PHD
author of *Trauma-Sensitive Mindfulness*

"Most books on this topic are either too new agey, too theoretical, or filled with motivational platitudes. *Wise Confidence* stands apart as a well-written and down-to-earth manual to self-transformation, grounded in ancient spiritual principles."

DHYANSE
author of *10 Bulls of Meditation*

"*Wise Confidence* is a masterfully creative synthesis of the most reliable practices from modern psychology, meditation, and spiritually based personal growth, all presented with very practical step-by-step instructions. It is also meticulously crafted, not a false or misleading note anywhere. The reader can take genuine ownership of the process. A real gem."

LINDA GRAHAM, MFT
psychotherapist and author of *Resilience*

T0006816

"In *Wise Confidence*, Giovanni invites you to embrace your aspirations and design your identity so you can authentically live from the inside out. The three pillars of self-confidence enable you to shift from self-doubt to self-belief and inner strength. This book emanates empowerment and peace—a rare and magical combination that fuels both greater success and fulfilment."

KATIE STODDART
leadership coach and speaker, author of *The Magic of Focus*

"In *Wise Confidence*, Giovanni has provided us with a wonderfully innovative and detailed approach to gaining confidence. He has shared the wisdom he has gained over his own life's journey, having been brought up in an environment that did not foster self-esteem or self-confidence. As a result of his inner search, he has given us the methods to develop a new self-image and inner power. The path outlined in the book cultivates the five elements of self-belief, courage, optimism, integrity, and determination. I highly recommend this book to anyone who is looking for a way to build greater inner strength and a more optimal way of navigating through the world."

DR. SWAMI SHANKARDEV SARASWATĪ
author of *The Practices of Yoga for the Digestive System*

"This book brings together tools from personal development, mindfulness, psychology, and wisdom traditions into a practical system that will help you build unshakable confidence and courage."

TAL LEEAD, PSYD
author of *Happier Being*

"*Wise Confidence* by Giovanni Dienstmann is your one-stop shop for turning self-doubt into self-belief. It's like a gym for your self-esteem, but instead of lifting weights, you're lifting your spirits with lessons from psychology, philosophy, spirituality, and mindfulness. So, if you're ready to flex your confidence muscles, this book is the personal trainer you didn't know you needed."

NICHOLAS STEIN, CMT-P
producer of National Geographic Channel's hit series *Border Wars*
and author of *Mindfulness as a Second Language*

"A fascinating, insightful, and practical book that will help you build unwavering self-confidence."

PATRIK EDBLAD
author of *The Self-Discipline Blueprint*

"This book masterfully combines actionable tools, inspiring stories, and ancient wisdom to help you find the best in yourself and live an inspiring life of confidence."

AZIZ GAZIPURA, PSYD
bestselling author of *The Art of Extraordinary Confidence*

"At getAbstract, we are always on the lookout for actionable tools to put wisdom into practice—and *Wise Confidence* provides them in spades. With reflection questions and suggested daily practices, Dienstmann guides you toward discovering who you want to be and acting in alignment with your aspirational identity. The book is practical, yet doesn't rely on hacks. It draws on academic research and spiritual concepts, yet presents them in an accessible framework. Dienstmann's previous book, *Mindful Self-Discipline*, has been a getAbstract customer favorite—and we can't wait to add the sequel to our library."

RAMONA MARCIONETTI
content manager for getAbstract

"This book is a game changer for anyone courageous enough to step into who they really are. Giovanni provides practical guidance for sensing your core presence, giving you the tools to shine with unshakable strength of heart and mind. This is his best book yet."

SEAN FARGO
founder of Mindfulness Exercises

"Deep and nuanced, yet practical and down to earth, this powerful book guides you to let go of your fear-based limitations and authentically step into your most confident self. Giovanni Dienstmann, once again, skillfully merges ancient wisdom with contemporary science, providing actionable guidance that will help you create unshakable confidence and turn your boldest aspirations into reality.

"As someone who has often struggled with quietening self-doubt and taking action, I won't hesitate to go back to this book when I need guidance, inspiration, or motivation to keep moving forward, fears and all!"

SHANNON JENKINS
podcast host and public speaking coach

WISE
CONFIDENCE

WISE
CONFIDENCE

Overcome Self-Doubt and Build Lasting Self-Esteem

GIOVANNI DIENSTMANN

sounds true
BOULDER, COLORADO

Sounds True
Boulder, CO

Published 2024

Cover design by Charli Barnes
Book design by Ranee Kahler

Printed in the United States of America

BK06712

Library of Congress Cataloging-in-Publication Data

Names: Dienstmann, Giovanni, author.
Title: Wise confidence : overcome self-doubt and build lasting self-esteem
    / Giovanni Dienstmann.
Description: Boulder, CO : Sounds True, Inc, 2024.
Identifiers: LCCN 2023026976 (print) | LCCN 2023026977 (ebook) | ISBN
    9781649631176 (paperback) | ISBN 9781649631183 (ebook)
Subjects: LCSH: Self-esteem. | Self-doubt. | Self-confidence.
Classification: LCC BF697.5.S46 D548 2024 (print) |
    LCC BF697.5.S46 (ebook) |
    DDC 158.1--dc23/eng/20230727
LC record available at https://lccn.loc.gov/2023026976
LC ebook record available at https://lccn.loc.gov/2023026977

FSC
www.fsc.org
MIX
Paper | Supporting
responsible forestry
FSC® C103098

Contents

Start Here

If I have lost confidence in myself, I have the universe against me.

—Ralph Waldo Emerson

Do you sometimes feel that you are playing too safe? Do you fear that if you continue like this life will pass you by, and your dreams will be left unfulfilled? Do you feel somewhat restricted by your limiting beliefs and thought patterns and wish you could feel more comfortable and empowered in your own skin, without being arrogant or cocky?

Imagine you had total confidence in yourself, in all areas of your life—in a way that is balanced and wise. What would you try? What possibilities would open up for you? How different would you feel from the inside?

Ask yourself this question: *What would I dare to pursue if I knew I could not fail?*

Are you pursuing that thing now? If not, a lack of self-confidence is likely the culprit. When you have greater confidence in yourself, you set bigger goals and live a bigger life.

Confidence is essential for both growth and well-being. Confidence is not arrogance—it is integrity. It is showing up as *one*, as a fully integrated, energized, and empowered individual. It is being on your own side, again and again. It is having unwavering faith in yourself, no matter what, knowing that you are capable of achieving what you aspire. It is taking bold steps, betting on potential, and working hard to fulfill it. It is being your authentic self and having fun with it.

The world has broken your self-confidence. Society has given you a mistaken idea about who you are and what you are capable of. If you are like most people, you have internalized that limiting identity, and now you live under the shadow of fear and self-doubt—the two biggest enemies of self-confidence. It is time to reclaim your power, your true self.

This book is an invitation for you to develop confidence from the inside out, instead of relying on hacks, empty formulas, and Band-Aid solutions. Not a confidence that comes with the side effects of conceit, unpreparedness, selfishness, impudence, and delusion. No. We're talking about a sense of confidence that is healthy, balanced, and deep. This is what I call *wise confidence*.

In this journey you'll develop a new self-image, powerful awareness tools, and a more optimal way of navigating the world. Aspiration, Awareness, and Action are, indeed, the three pillars of self-confidence. There might be genetic, environmental, or traumatic factors that make self-confidence difficult for you, but none of that can stop you. Once you digest and implement the three pillars, you'll have a core of confidence that will make the other factors irrelevant.

MY STORY: I SHOULDN'T BE CONFIDENT, BUT I AM

Some people never have any issues with self-confidence. They were born to parents who supported their dreams, cherished their presence, complimented their skills, celebrated their successes, and helped them build up a core of self-love and self-belief. Other people had to deal with more adverse environments—an overcritical parent, emotional manipulation, bullying at school, or a dominating family member.

In the first case, as you are shaping your personality, everything around you is sending you encouraging messages: "You are good. You are worth it. Your opinions and desires matter. You can do anything you set your mind to." In the second case, your environment is shaping the opposite beliefs in you: "You're not good enough. You are worth nothing. What you think or feel doesn't matter. You are alone."

The environment I grew up in was more akin to the latter. I had a narcissistic mother—unpleasable, dominating, and emotionally unavailable.

A mother who panicked and yelled for no good reason, who was more concerned about arbitrary household rules than our well-being, and who always had a word of criticism to offer when what we needed was encouragement. On top of that, being a shy and skinny kid, and relatively short for my age, made me a target of repeated bullying at school. That was the hand of cards I was dealt.

To be fair, not all was bad, and I know many people have it much worse. We did have financial support, and we were taken to classes we were interested in, like piano, English, swimming, and karate lessons. But the fact remains that emotionally and psychologically I was on my own. I had to raise myself. Self-esteem and self-confidence were not given—they had to be won.

Realizing this fact was the turning point for me. I don't know how or why, but when I was about nine years old, something inside of me woke up and said, This is not who I am. I am strong. I am valuable. The world may be against me, but from now on I will choose to always be on my side. I'll take care of myself.

That moment was more of an internal shift rather than an inner dialogue. The words were not fully articulated, but that was the underlying feeling. Even though I didn't know it at that time, I was beginning the process of *living from the inside out*. I was throwing away the need for external validation, and instead choosing who I wanted to be. In a way, that was the beginning of this book.

I share this personal story to make a simple point. Whatever your past and upbringing, there is a possibility open for you: you can reinvent yourself. You can find out who you are, or choose who you want to be, and live your life in alignment with that purpose, from the *inside out*, regardless of the conditions around you.

Given my upbringing, I should be struggling with self-confidence and self-worth. In fact, several of the people who have come to me for coaching have had a similar past, and they were not in a place of confidence and well-being. Some were struggling with crippling anxiety, others with self-doubt or self-sabotage, and almost everybody with an overbearing inner critic.

So here is the thing: your past doesn't need to determine your future. Changing your core conditioning won't be easy, of course, but it's possible and extremely valuable. To embark on this journey, all that is required is a deep desire to change and a willingness to take full responsibility for your healing and your growth. In my case, I refused to be a victim or see myself as a victim. I took ownership of my life, of my purpose, and of my happiness. It is my sincere hope that you are ready to do that too.

WHAT'S DIFFERENT ABOUT THIS BOOK

I've read several books on self-confidence, and in general terms they all emphasize three things: reframing negative thoughts, facing your fears, and applying quick fixes to feel more confident in the moment. But there is much more to it than that; these topics are just three of the chapters in this book.

Wise Confidence puts together several effective approaches for developing confidence in a concise, comprehensive, and accessible framework. It combines lessons from psychology, mindfulness, spirituality, and personal growth literature. This book goes deep yet remains completely practical. It is based on research, but it's not an academic read. It is inspired by spiritual insights, but it's not a mystical book. It will give you some work to do; it is not about Band-Aid solutions or pop psychology feel-good platitudes. It's also not the "yelling in your face" type of motivational book.

The framework covered in this book, with the underlying concept of *living inside out*, is applicable not only to self-confidence but to any self-transformation journey. This is especially true for chapters 5 to 13.

My purpose here is to give you everything I've got in the space available. I'll hold nothing back. That said, there are further resources that can't be included in a book—such as guided meditations, personal mentoring, and interactive tools—and when the shift we are discussing could benefit from one of these, I'll let you know where to go to learn more.

I'm a spiritual guy, so you will see references to concepts from spiritual traditions here and there. They will be briefly explained in the text so we keep the focus on the main conversation. If you are not familiar with them, don't worry; this doesn't harm your comprehension and practice of the book. But if they do resonate with you, they'll add a layer of meaning and impact to the work.

The order of the chapters in this book was chosen purposefully. We'll start with the most fundamental work, your identity, and build up from there. This is the first pillar. The other two pillars complement and consolidate the foundational work, and they can also be used as stand-alone tools. Different things work for different people, so explore freely and find what works for you. (For a quick overview of the pillars, see chapter 4.)

Self-confidence is a skill that can be learned—a skill that YOU can learn. This book was created to be the best manual you can find. It was not designed to be the first self-confidence book you read. It was designed to be the last.

Let's begin.

PART 1

THE FUNDAMENTALS

1.

What Is Wise Confidence?

The whole problem with the world is that fools and fanatics
are always so certain of themselves,
and wiser people so full of doubts.

—Bertrand Russell

Half the battle is in the conviction
that we can do what we undertake.

—Orison Swett Marden

Trust thyself: every heart vibrates to that iron string.

—Ralph Waldo Emerson

What do you think of when you hear the term *self-confidence*? Do you associate it with self-assurance, self-esteem, and self-belief? Or do you associate it more with arrogance, pretentiousness, bravado, ego, and conceit?

Perhaps you feel that being unapologetically confident means fooling yourself and taking too many risks, leaving life to eventually give you a painful "correction." Many people believe that self-doubt is a sign of intelligence and that having confidence and optimism makes one "naïve." Others believe that with confidence comes an overbearing or domineering personality, that we become selfish or even aggressive. You may also have a sense that self-confidence goes against your spiritual beliefs, practices, or goals. Some of us may subconsciously reject confidence because we don't want to step on other people's toes or take up too much space. Believing in yourself and fighting for what you want may go against years of ingrained conditioning and against the image others have of you.

Does any of this resonate? If you lack self-confidence, it is likely that you have some resistance toward becoming more confident. The purpose of this chapter is to show you a different approach to self-confidence and to give you a model of confidence that you can say a wholehearted "yes" to. I call it Wise Confidence.

THE FIVE ELEMENTS OF SELF-CONFIDENCE

When you have self-confidence, you believe in yourself, and you show up to every challenge in life with courage, optimism, integrity, and determination. When you lack self-confidence, you fall into its opposites: fear, pessimism, insecurity, and self-doubt.

Let's unpack these concepts.

Self-confidence is, first of all, an act of self-belief. The opposite of self-belief is self-doubt.

When you doubt yourself, you give away your power. You think that you can't do things, that you are not good enough, that you "shouldn't," that your goals will "never happen." You hesitate and cannot meet the challenge at hand with your full capacity.

Self-doubt prevents you from jumping in wholeheartedly by telling you that you don't have the needed skills, intelligence, time, resources, or experience to get the job done. You defeat yourself before you even try. And while it's true that self-belief may not guarantee success, self-doubt often guarantees failure.

Self-confidence is your ability to believe that you can accomplish the task ahead of you, regardless of the difficulties. It is the unshakable conviction that you can do anything you put your mind to. It is betting on yourself, betting on success, and at the same time knowing that you can stomach any failure. It is often a result of being aware of your strengths, skills, and potential.

It is easy to be confident when we are making progress and achieving goals. But our confidence easily shakes when we experience setbacks, especially if repeatedly. If you don't want your self-confidence to be shaken by failures, you need to cultivate a sense of self-worth that is not dependent on any particular person or outcome. It needs to be based on something essential—something within you that transcends circumstance. There may be uncertainty in the outcome, but there is no longer uncertainty in yourself. (You'll learn more about this in later chapters of this book.)

The second element of self-confidence is courage. The opposite is being held back by fear. Courage is always being ready to face the world, no matter what challenges life brings. With courage, you believe that if a challenge comes your way, it's because you *can* overcome it, in one way or another. And as a result, you face it with full energy.

When you trust your capacity, you are motivated to take action, and you have the strength to face your fears and move forward. When you are confident, you naturally act more courageous; when you act based on courage, you naturally become more confident.

Self-confidence is the willingness to take steps toward goals that you care about, even when doing so makes you anxious. So it has the virtue of courage built in.

The third element of self-confidence is optimism. Its opposite is negativity.

When we feel confident, we know what we are capable of, and we anticipate being successful. The word confidence comes from the Latin word *confidere*, meaning "with trust." Acting with trust usually means we are not completely certain of the outcome, yet we choose to take a leap of faith and bet on a positive result.

It is very hard to be confident if your mind is filled with thoughts about how things will go wrong. When that is your mindset, you are emphasizing the obstacles, challenges, and risks, assuming they will be greater than your capacity to overcome them. Optimism is, thus, contained in confidence and is a *fuel* for confidence. When you fully trust your capacity, you are optimistic; on the other hand, when you are optimistic, you tend to trust your skills more.

The fourth element of self-confidence is integrity. The opposites are self-criticism and self-sabotage.

The word *integrity* means "being whole and undivided." For the purposes of self-confidence, having integrity means that the *whole* of you is moving forward. In other words, there is no part inside yourself that is sabotaging the action you want to take.

Being *whole* means you do not second-guess yourself, beat yourself up, argue for your limitations, or mentally defeat yourself before you even begin. Instead, you are on your own side. No part of you is saying that you shouldn't be doing this or that you won't succeed. Instead, you show up as *one*.

Integrity results in you being wholeheartedly focused. When there is no internal contradiction in you, when you believe in yourself rather than doubt yourself, only then can you show up for the challenge with your full capacity.

When you fully believe in yourself, you are *one*—all parts of you are on the same team. When you doubt yourself, you are two—your energy is divided and conflicting. Self-confidence is about being one, undivided.

The fifth and final element of self-confidence is determination, or willpower. Its opposites are hesitation, passivity, weakness, and inertia.

Confidence requires you to believe that you can exert some level of control over the environment, yourself, and your outcomes. If you believe you have no free will or that everything is pre-determined, you can't really be confident that your actions will matter. Similarly, if you believe your actions matter but you are not really committed to the change you want to make, you'll likely not feel very confident that it will happen.

When you act with wise confidence—meaning you are not just fooling yourself and being naïve—there is an internal resolve to move forward despite competing stimuli. This is willpower. It includes your capacity to override unwanted thoughts and feelings and shift your internal state. The willpower aspect of confidence is the dynamic conviction that says, "I *must* succeed," "I *can*," and "Sooner or later, I *will*." It is a form of inner commitment or resolve. Fill every corner of your mind with such determination, and there will be no space left for self-doubt.

In the philosophical tradition of Yoga and Hindu Tantra, confidence is seen as an expression of the power of the mind, called *manas shakti*. Confidence, willpower, concentration, and faith are all expressions of the power of our mind. When led by any of these, you experience determination, courage, motivation, and heightened energy. You feel comfortable holding fast to your values and goals, and you are not easily shaken. You are then willing to commit to the task at hand and pay the price of achievement.

Can you feel the fire that comes from that?

Some people may experience resistance or confusion with willpower's statement of "I must." Here, "must" is not something that comes from outside of you and forces you to do something. It's also not a form of conditioning that says you have to do something to become "good enough" in the eyes of others (or of yourself). "I must" is a *choice*. It is you focusing all your energy on a single goal, with full conviction and commitment. When you feel the power of "I must," you create a concentration of energy that naturally fills you with confidence. This is something that is hard to express in words—it needs to be experienced.

"I must" does not go against your free will; rather, it's an expression of it. "I must" is a feeling that's consciously created from within. It's voluntarily relinquishing all other options, to generate focus. It is letting go of a plan B so that all your energy can only go to plan A. When you *decide* "I must do this" or "I must succeed" with this understanding, you give yourself no other option but to show up as your best. Therefore, you do.

"I'd like to" is a preference. "I'd love to" is a wish. "I want to" is a desire. "I must" is focus and commitment. Higher than that is "I will," which is determination and self-belief—a resolution.

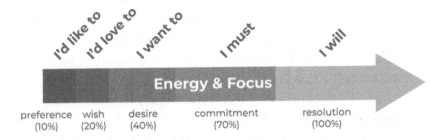

Let's make this more concrete. Think of a change you want to make in yourself or in your life. Now try framing it in a sentence using these different levels of commitment, and read each of these sentences to yourself. Observe how they all affect you differently and evoke different emotions.

> I'd like to become a great designer.
>
> I'd love to become a great designer.
>
> I want to become a great designer.
>
> I must become a great designer.
>
> I will become a great designer.

Where you are in the commitment scale determines your level of energy, motivation, and focus. If there is no resolution but just a mild desire mixed with self-doubt, you won't generate enough energy to accomplish anything big or to overcome difficult challenges. You'll only have enough energy to accomplish things that are easy, and therefore you'll feel small and not so capable.

Let's use the analogy of electricity to further illustrate this point. Think of your brain as a lamp with potential for infinite brightness and your intention or willpower as the current. When you just have a soft intention to do something, the amount of energy you create is low—let's say, 30 volts. Consequently, the current that passes through your brain is also low, and the amount of light you produce is small. That limits what you can see and what you can do. On the other hand, when you have full determination to accomplish something, you generate a much higher amount of energy—let's say, 200 volts. As a result, the current powering your brain is much higher; it activates more resources and produces more light. You feel more capable, more confident, more *charged*.

As a concentrated form of willpower, a resolution is that higher voltage that helps you tap into deeper resources within you. It makes the *whole* of you come alive. With that, believing in yourself and moving forward with courage in the face of challenges becomes much easier.

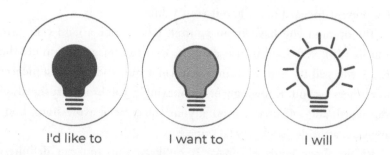

I'd like to   I want to   I will

We have now covered the five aspects of self-confidence: determination, integrity, self-belief, courage, and optimism. Which of these elements are already strong for you? And which one(s) do you need to work on the most, to become more confident?

Let's now see how self-confidence differs from related terms with which it is often confused.

SELF-ESTEEM, SELF-EFFICACY, AND SELF-CONFIDENCE

Self-esteem encompasses how you feel about yourself both individually and as it relates to your role in the world. It answers the questions, "Do I like myself?" and "Am I good?" It is your sense of self-worth, significance, or personal value, and it tends to be more of an enduring trait, rather than a state of being.

The most famous conceptualization and theory of self-esteem is from Abraham Maslow, who argued that there are two kinds of self-esteem: a "higher" one and a "lower" one. The lower self-esteem comes from the respect shown to you by others, while the higher self-esteem comes from within you.

Self-esteem and self-confidence usually overlap—if you have positive feelings about yourself, you probably also have positive feelings about your capacity. However, that is not always so. You could hate yourself yet also have confidence in what you can do. Or you could love yourself but lack belief in your capacity. Self-confidence is more of a forward-looking belief about your capacity, while self-esteem is more of a present-focused belief about your value.

The opinion you have about yourself tends to be a hard ceiling in your life; it is very hard to rise above it. Your self-image determines the things you will try and the things you will avoid, and it also influences how others see you. Knowingly or unknowingly, you broadcast signals of your worth and self-image through your voice, facial expressions, body language, attitudes, and general "vibe."

Rising above your self-image is unlikely. But you can definitely change it through the work discussed in this book.

Self-efficacy is a more context-specific assessment of your competence. It answers the question, "Can I do this?" In other words, it's self-confidence for a specific skill or situation. Your self-efficacy is influenced by your history of successes and failures, vicarious experiences (seeing others succeed at a similar thing), self-talk, visualization, emotional states, and moods.

The term was coined by the psychologist Albert Bandura, who suggested that your expectations of efficacy are the major reasons for your choice of activity, the effort you put into it, the degree of persistence you show, and your general motivation. If you don't think you will succeed at something, you are unlikely to start it or to continue it for long.

As your skill in a particular activity increases and you get some wins under your belt, your confidence for performing *that activity* increases, but this doesn't mean you become more confident in general. That confidence may not be transferable to any other area of your life. But if you work on your self-confidence as a whole, then your self-efficacy in all areas of life gets a boost. More about this in a moment.

In a nutshell, self-confidence is how much you trust yourself, believe in yourself, and are willing to bet on yourself. It is your general perception of your abilities combined with your tendency to believe in your capacity, skills, judgments, and likelihood of success in your endeavors. It's a set of enduring positive beliefs, self-talk, and self-image. It creates a buffer against life's challenges. Most people equate it with self-belief, which is one of its predominant elements.

Wise confidence cannot depend on you having already succeeded at a particular task—that is self-efficacy. At any given time, there are countless challenges that you have not yet faced, skills you have not yet developed, tasks you have not yet completed, and things you have not yet learned. So self-confidence cannot depend on previous successes or experiences—albeit it is definitely enhanced by them. It is, rather, an *a priori* attitude, an inclination to believe in yourself no matter what. It's tied in with your identity and self-talk and is thus more sustainable.

When you have this type of confidence, there is something inside of you that says, *No matter what life throws at me, I'll be able to handle it.* It is impossible for you to feel anxious if you *truly* believe this statement. Not because you naively think that things will always turn out the way you expect, but because you trust your capacity so much that you just don't need to be afraid.

Successful people not only have confidence
that they will eventually succeed, but are equally confident
that they will have a tough time getting there.

—Heidi Grant Halvorson

Competence vs. Self-Belief

Now that we have covered the key concepts of self-confidence, we can talk about one of its most common misconceptions: the idea that you can only be confident if you are actually good at doing something—that otherwise you're fooling yourself. This misconception exists because people often confuse competence (self-efficacy) with confidence (self-belief).

When you have practiced a given skill or developed a certain quality to a high degree, you naturally feel confident about it. But that is different from being a confident person in general. Confidence in your *skills* comes as a result of practice; confidence in *yourself* is a matter of self-belief and self-talk.

Improving skills builds confidence but also *takes* confidence. You won't do it if you don't believe you can. So don't depend on skills to build your confidence; rather, use your confidence to build your skills.

If you believe that confidence only comes from previous successes and achievements, then you are severely limiting yourself. Self-confidence is not the result of you being an amazing person, acquiring many skills, and enjoying success across all areas of life. It is the *cause* of all of this. It is not the final profit of a long-term investment—it is the initial deposit.

No matter how much competence you develop in any skill or area of life, the monkey-mind can always bring up doubts, arguing that you are "never good enough." This type of insecurity then pushes you to work harder, get more credentials, or overcompensate your self-doubt with external accomplishments and status symbols—often pursuing goals that are not really aligned with your deeper values. On the other hand, the type of confidence we are talking about in this book is confidence in your *core*. It is based on who you are—your identity, personal values, qualities, and self-talk. It is how you choose to navigate the world. It is how you see yourself.

Competence is important. It is something worth pursuing, but it doesn't replace the need to do the internal work that develops self-confidence in your core. The strongest, deepest, and most reliable form of confidence is based on identity and mindset—not skills, experiences, looks, or moods. It is your unwavering choice to believe in yourself, to be on your own side, to show up with full energy, courage, and optimism to every challenge, *no matter what.*

This confidence is unshakable because it doesn't depend on any particular condition. If your confidence is conditional on something external to yourself, then it will fade away as soon as that condition is removed. Doubt can also arise about the validity of that condition—prompted either by your inner critic or by people around you. If, on the other hand, your confidence is *transcendental* and based on self-belief, then nothing can shake it. As long as you are still choosing to believe in yourself and in your capacity, you are still confident. Period.

Competence is objective—either you have the skill or you don't. Confidence is subjective—it is an expression of your self-image and self-belief. They are both important, but self-confidence takes precedence. No amount of skill or success can fully compensate for a broken self-image. You can layer skill after skill on top of a foundation of self-doubt and it will never feel like it's enough. Impostor syndrome is not overcome this way. You may have great skill in a given activity, but if you feel bad about yourself and are too demoralized to make use of it, your skill will amount to nothing.

THE WAY OF WISE CONFIDENCE

Wise Confidence is a balanced approach to confidence. It brings in the elements of wisdom, awareness, and humility to remove the excesses of ego from self-confidence. It's a more mindful and evolved way of expressing this important virtue.

At one extreme we have lack of confidence, or self-doubt. Here, you are anxious about the fruits of your efforts. There is no certainty fueling your actions. As a result, you may not take a step forward—or if you do, it's half-hearted, hesitant, and weak. You don't have the motivation and energy needed to power through the obstacles that show up and to persevere in difficult times. In a way, you are living a low-voltage life.

At the other extreme is overconfidence, or arrogance. You have plenty of certainty, motivation, energy, and boldness—but you are blinded. You can't see your biases, you don't prepare for contingencies, you expect quick results, you are unaware of your shortcomings, and your optimism is unrealistic. This is the confidence of bullies, narcissists, and egomaniacs, and is an aspect of what is modernly known as toxic masculinity.

For some people, such overconfidence is a natural part of who they are; for others, it is something they pretend via looks, body language, affirmations, and status symbols to compensate for their underlying insecurities. They do this because they desire the obvious benefits of being and looking confident, but they are unaware of the pitfalls of overconfidence. Life will eventually pull the rug from under their feet.

With overconfidence, you overestimate your abilities or underestimate the magnitude of the task in front of you. Neither of these things is beneficial, as they increase the likelihood of failure and disappointment. Overconfidence, or cockiness, is when you think you are so good that you don't need to prepare, don't need to try hard, and cannot fail. As a result, you are not fully present—half of you has already checked out.

Overconfidence limits your growth in life because it makes it harder for you to acknowledge your faults, shortcomings, and ignorance. How can you learn if you think you know it all? It also makes you less patient and less willing to "start small" and baby-step through the process.

The balanced approach is Wise Confidence. You have a healthy dose of respect for the path ahead, awareness of your strengths, and awareness of your shortcomings. You know there will be challenges, yet you believe in your capacity and have the determination to overcome them. You move forward with full self-belief, courage, optimism, integrity, and willpower.

You choose to show up as your best self, suspending doubts and negative self-talk. You bet that you will succeed on the task at hand, and yet you also know how to get up and try again after failure.

Both in self-doubt and in overconfidence, you are absorbed in thinking about yourself, whether it's "I suck" or "I'm great." But with Wise Confidence you are not busy judging yourself; rather, you are focused on showing up with courage, energy, and integrity.

Wise Confidence doesn't mean that you believe you'll be flawless, can do no wrong, and will always succeed—that is foolishness. It also doesn't involve feeling that you are better than others. It is simply an unshakable belief in yourself and your infinite potential.

Let me give you an example from the world of martial arts. Suppose you need to face an opponent who is bigger, stronger, and meaner than you. "Opponent" here is a metaphor for any challenge in your life. What attitude would be most helpful?

If you are in self-doubt mode, you'll think, *Oh, this is not going to end well for me. He is stronger than me. How can I overcome this? I have no chance.* You are divided. The match hasn't even started yet, and you are already defeating yourself. Your energy and strength are dissipated. When you think victory is unlikely, you won't fight with all your might.

If you are in overconfidence mode, you'll think, *No problem, I've got this; I'll easily beat him up because I'm better.* In this case, you are not divided, but deluded. You underestimate the challenge and therefore will not be able to harness your whole capacity to deal with it. When you think you can win with little effort, you won't fight with all your might.

Now, in the mode of Wise Confidence, you'll think: *I'm fully present to this challenge, and I'll show up with my best self. I trust my capacity and my skill. I'll tap into all I've got. I must succeed in this. It has to happen. I'm determined to show up with all I am, regardless of the outcome. I'm not afraid of him—he should be afraid of me.* Here, you're showing up undivided, with full courage and determination, and with empowering self-talk. You're neither underestimating the challenge (overconfidence) nor underestimating yourself (self-doubt).

Self-Doubt	Overconfidence	Wise Confidence
anxious about outcome	baseless conviction	healthy self-belief
divided	undivided but blinded	whole and clear
avoiding	audacious	courageous
hesitant	impulsive	energetic
humble	cocky	humble yet strong
pessimism	deluded optimism	wise optimism
overprepared	underprepared	cautious yet bold
underestimate yourself	underestimate the challenges	aware yet determined
focused on one's faults	unaware of one's faults	aware yet optimistic
not fully present	not fully present	fully present
not tapping into your full capacity due to doubt	not tapping into your full capacity due to arrogance	showing up with full integrity, energy, focus
defeat yourself before even facing the challenge	declare victory before even facing the challenge	face the challenge with self-belief, courage, optimism
no confidence	egotistical confidence	balanced confidence

Take a moment to think of a challenge in your life where you'd like to have more confidence. Contemplate how you can show up with wise confidence in it.

It is wise to believe in yourself. It is also wise to be humble. This is Wise Confidence. And it's a skill that can be learned. It is something that you *practice*.

2.

Why Confidence Matters

Nothing splendid has ever been achieved
except by those who dared believe
that something inside of them
was superior to circumstance.

—Bruce Barton

Believe in yourself
and the world will be at your feet.

—Swami Vivekananda

Y ou likely chose this book because you have a sense of how important self-confidence is and how it can positively impact your life. Let's expand on that understanding, because the more you are aware of the benefits of confidence, the more motivation you will have to go through the journey of developing it.

THE PAINS OF SELF-DOUBT

When you lack self-confidence, you second-guess yourself frequently, apologize excessively, ruminate on your mistakes, and don't take risks due to fear of failure. Doing so places a low ceiling above your head, for self-doubt will not allow you to pursue certain goals or dreams. As a result, you tend to stay in your comfort zone and not grow much.

In relationships and social interactions, you may feel the desperate need to accommodate others and fit in, even at the cost of your authenticity. You may also be perceived as needy, fragile, and insecure. Some lesser-evolved people may even see you as someone who can be taken advantage of.

There may be an internal sense of being an impostor and some nagging thoughts of not being good enough. You then tend to work really hard to prove yourself worthy and overprepare for everything. But doing this doesn't really solve the issue because the problem is not a lack of effort, but an unhealthy self-image and negative self-talk.

With self-doubt also comes a sense of anxiety and powerlessness. The world can feel like a scary and frustrating place when you feel that you can't pursue your goals effectively, fulfill your needs, or influence the course of events in your life. Self-doubt kills joy, creativity, and purpose. Your larger life is waiting for you, on the other side of self-doubt.

THE BENEFITS OF SELF-CONFIDENCE

When you have self-confidence, you take action on your goals because you know that success is possible. You start important projects, take meaningful risks, and have the resilience to persevere through challenges. You procrastinate less because you no longer fear failure. You finish what you start.

Self-confidence is, thus, an essential ingredient for self-actualization. It's often the bridge between *aspiring* to do something and actually *doing* it, between starting something and continuing it until the end. We all operate differently when we feel sure we can succeed versus when we just think we *might*. Confidence invites us to show up with that greater conviction and energy.

Confidence also helps you perform better in almost any area of life, whether it's your studies, sports, work, relationships, or business. It makes it more likely that you will overcome any challenges in your path, for confidence boosts your resilience, willpower, and motivation.

In relationships, being confident means you are not driven by a fear of rejection, nor do you feel the urge to go against your needs and values to please others. You feel comfortable stating what you need and setting boundaries. When you believe in yourself and want the best for yourself, the way you interact with others and who you choose to have in your life will change.

Social interactions also flow more easily when you have self-confidence. Since you are not busy with thoughts of self-doubt, you can be more present with the person in front of you. Everything flows more naturally and is more pleasant because you are not engaging from a place of insecurity or anxiety.

At work, confident people more easily get the trust and cooperation of their peers, bosses, customers, and audiences. On the flip side, uncertainty begets uncertainty. If you habitually doubt yourself, so will others. No one will follow a leader who appears unsure of him- or herself. A study by the University of Sussex found that we're biologically wired to respect the opinions of confident people more than insecure people.[1]

With self-confidence you'll do better at job interviews, and once you're in the job, you'll likely progress more quickly because confidence highlights competence. Self-confidence also makes you more influential and persuasive, which is an essential skill in many lines of work.

In terms of mental and emotional well-being, self-confidence diminishes overthinking, which is associated with anxiety and depression. Your inner critic becomes more manageable, you have fewer negative thoughts, and you feel better about yourself.

With greater confidence you also:

- are more willing to try new things, since you're not afraid of failing

- are more optimistic about your future, since you feel you can influence it

- welcome new chapters of your life with less anxiety

- become more resilient, since you have faith in your ability to grow and recover

- recover from illness more quickly, since your immune system is stronger[2]

- are perceived as more attractive and valuable by others

- feel more in control of your life

There are also important links between confidence and motivation. Motivation is your emotional fuel to take a certain action, and it depends on three elements: high reward, high chance of success, and low friction (meaning that the process of achieving the reward is not more painful than the reward itself). The reward might be huge, but if you doubt you will succeed, you are less likely to take action.

With greater self-confidence comes greater certainty of success. This means you will take action on the things that matter to you—even if the path ahead is difficult and the outcome uncertain.

As you can see, confidence is linked to almost every element of a happy and fulfilling life.

Exercise: Self-Confidence Audit

Let's take a moment to make all of this more concrete for you. I invite you to get a pen and some paper—or open a note-taking app—and reflect on the following:

- In what areas of your life are you already confident?

- In what areas of your life do you lack confidence the most?

- What opportunities have you turned down in life because you didn't feel confident enough? List at least five.

- What goals would you pursue if you had more confidence? Think of the different areas of life, such as health, career, relationships, lifestyle, or finances.

- What are three things you would try if you had full self-belief and no fear of failure?

If you carefully reflect on these questions, you will feel, deeply, how important this journey is for you. Expand that feeling, and it will fill you with the motivation, purpose, and determination you need.

For some of us, self-confidence is a revolutionary choice. Get excited by that possibility. Allow that feeling to fuel you forward.

3.

What Stands in Your Way

Never say "no," never say "I cannot"
for you are infinite.
All the power is within you.
You can do anything.

—Swami Vivekananda

Where does lack of self-confidence come from? Why do some people struggle with this, and others don't? Understanding the origin of this problem is not a requirement for overcoming it, but many people find that it brings a helpful amount of clarity. Let's dive in and see what we can find.

CAUSES OF LOW SELF-CONFIDENCE

The most common reason for a lack of self-confidence is childhood conditioning. The way people around us saw us and treated us, especially in our early years, had a formative effect on our personality. If you grew up with unsupportive parents, constant criticism from friends and family, bullying, or discrimination, you likely internalized a disempowering self-image. If whenever you tried to do something and failed you got harsh emotional reactions from others, then you would feel that failure is dangerous and that you shouldn't try new things. If your parents were overprotective of you due to their own fears, that may have sent you a repeated message that the world is a dangerous place and you can't take care of yourself.

A second cause of low self-confidence may be that it's a side effect of a personal trait. Perhaps you are cautious and reserved by nature, and don't tend to take risks or act boldly. Perhaps you are a perfectionist, which can contribute to you feeling like you're never good enough. It could even be that, due to your genetic makeup, you tend to produce less serotonin, oxytocin, or dopamine—the confidence-boosting chemicals.

A third reason you may experience low self-confidence is due to comparisons. In the age of social media and ubiquitous advertisement, this is a particularly pervasive issue.

> *One reason we struggle with insecurity:*
> *we're comparing our behind-the-scenes*
> *to everyone else's highlight reel.*
>
> —Steven Furtick

Self-confidence is about who you are at your core, and not about your position in the social hierarchy or how you compare with others. I call this "living inside out," a concept we will explore at length in the coming chapters.

When you are concerned about what others think of you and how they judge you, you are living "outside in," relying on external validation to determine how confident you have the right to feel. If your confidence is thus tied to other people's perceptions, it will be fragile and unstable.

The media doesn't help either. Companies that want to sell you products via ads usually do so by making you feel bad about yourself, often by introducing a problem. They create a gap between where you see yourself and where they suggest you should be. Likewise, following social media stars and influencers can lead to the comparison trap and create feelings of being less than.

Depending on who you compare yourself to, your self-confidence will increase or decrease. This is known as the big-fish-little-pond effect: if you're a good student in a mediocre class, you'll feel smarter than if you're merely a good student in a class of geniuses. In both classes your skills are the same, yet your self-image is different due to comparisons. Does that mean you should seek environments where you can be the smartest one in the room, so you feel good about yourself? No. But it does mean you need to be aware of the effects of comparisons on your self-esteem and self-confidence, and be wise about the thoughts you believe in.

Comparing yourself to others is not necessarily bad. It can be a way to motivate you, for example, when you admire the skill, position, or knowledge of somebody else and believe you can also get there. But comparisons become disempowering if they make you think you are not good enough because you are "not there yet." So, comparisons can be a power or a poison, depending on your mindset (we'll talk about this more in chapter 9).

The fourth possible cause of low self-confidence is the company you keep. As Jim Rohn used to say, we are the average of the five people we spend the most time with. If some of these people are stuck in blaming, victimization, or other disempowering thoughts, or if they are condescending toward you or don't believe in your capacity, there will be a strong unconscious force undermining your self-confidence.

The fact is some people don't want you to succeed. Not necessarily because they are malevolent (although that could be the case). Maybe they just envy you. Maybe your progress highlights their feelings of inadequacy. Maybe they think *they* don't deserve to go after certain goals, and they feel triggered that you dare try to get those things yourself. Maybe they just don't believe that your goal is worthy, good, or possible. They may even appear selfless and concerned, trying to dissuade you from following your dreams so that you don't meet disappointment.

Deep down, some people in your life may not want you to be confident. Confidence is a form of power, and you having that power may highlight their insecurities. Your lack of self-confidence is also very profitable for thousands of companies because when you are in a disempowered state, they can more easily sell you products that promise you a quick fix to feel better.

People who want to disempower you may use many tactics. One of the most common is shaming. Shaming is a potent form of emotional manipulation that almost always puts you in a state where you feel you need to defend yourself to uphold your self-image. This is a virus for self-confidence. Instead of standing strong in who you are, you are now busy trying to prove you are not a bad person. They have effectively used shame to control you.

In chapter 17 we'll talk about how to deal with toxic people and their emotional games. For now, it suffices to be aware that some forces in your life may not want you to be confident. So don't wait for the world to give you permission to be confident. Take it yourself.

Another cause for low self-confidence is experiencing a big failure without knowing how to process it properly. Perhaps you had good self-confidence and high self-esteem and did well in life, until one day you fell and hit the ground *hard*. That can be a traumatizing experience, after which it becomes hard for you to bet on yourself again. You internalized not only the lesson from that failure but also a more defeatist self-image. There may now be a voice inside of you that always tells you to play it safe. It is trying to protect you by keeping you away from any risk of further pain.

Lack of self-confidence can also be a result of a lack of self-discipline. If you keep breaking your commitments to yourself, skipping your positive habits, not taking action on your goals, not finishing what you start, and giving in to unhelpful temptations, then your self-image will suffer. You'll like yourself less. You will feel less in control, less empowered, less capable.

Self-discipline is one of the best ways of developing confidence. Every time you keep your promises to yourself despite adverse circumstances, and every time you work hard on difficult but important goals, you make a deposit in your emotional bank account of self-esteem and self-confidence. When you are disciplined you feel powerful, effective, and focused. You know, experientially, that you can accomplish difficult goals and make positive changes in your life.

Therefore, learning how to be more disciplined, and, thus, live in alignment with your values, also supports you in developing self-confidence. For a deep dive on this topic, you can refer to my book *Mindful Self-Discipline*.

Finally, it's important to be aware that if you have gone through traumatizing experiences in your past and these are at the core of your challenges with self-confidence, you will likely need the support of a mental health professional who specializes in trauma to help you process those experiences. The framework in this book will still be valuable in your journey, yet it provides a different kind of inner work. You may need both to fully move forward.

IDENTIFYING SELF-SABOTAGE

If you have tried many times to be more confident and failed, it's likely because part of you doesn't want to be confident. In other words, lack of confidence may have hidden benefits for you.

What on earth could be the benefit of having low self-confidence? Well, it "protects" you from failure. It gives you the perfect excuse to not go beyond your comfort zone—and thus keeps you safe from difficult feelings that you may not know how to face, such as disappointment, rejection, shame, vulnerability, or regret. Depending on your life history and personality makeup, these secondary benefits might speak louder than the benefits of being confident. As a result, there is internal conflict in you: a part of you wants confidence and another part is afraid of it.

So let me ask: What could go wrong if you choose to believe in yourself more? Take your time. It is worth reflecting on this deeply, for it is the biggest of all obstacles.

MOVING FORWARD

What are your biggest challenges when it comes to self-confidence? Which of the causes listed in this chapter resonated with you the most?

Getting clear on this can help you better digest and implement the tools outlined in the rest of this book.

You may have identified more than one cause that's contributing to your low self-confidence. Maybe they are all present for you in some form. Even if that's the case, please don't panic. With the help of the tools in this book, you will be creating a new foundation for yourself. And remember, the shift toward self-confidence brings many benefits with it, and is worth every effort!

It doesn't matter where you are starting from; all that matters is where you are going.

> *Do what you can,*
> *with what you have,*
> *where you are.*

—Theodore Roosevelt

After reading this chapter, perhaps you believe that your lack of confidence is not really your fault. You may not have started this problem, but one thing is certain: you have the power to end it. And only you can. Nobody else can do it for you.

Make a commitment now to overcome this challenge once and for all. Commit to walking this path and taking care of yourself. Our first responsibility is to take good care of ourselves. Only when we can do that effectively can we be a real force of good in the world.

In the next chapter, we'll dive into the Three Pillars, which together are the answer to all these self-confidence challenges.

4.

The Three Pillars of Self-Confidence

There are countless ways to increase your self-confidence. Some of them are quick-acting yet superficial; others are slow burners but bring deeper shifts. Some of them work on the level of your self-image, while others create empowering feelings or aim to overcome negative self-talk. The Three Pillars framework is a way to organize all these approaches into a single cohesive system and is based on the larger framework of my teaching, Mindful Self-Discipline.

The first pillar is Aspiration, which is all about knowing who you are, knowing what you want, and *living inside out* from your strengths and vision. It is first showing up as your best self (expressing core strengths), then designing and embodying your aspirational identity (the new you). This pillar also includes tools for overcoming the conditioned identity—such as self-acceptance, clarifying fears, and the ROAR Method for releasing negative emotions. I'll also provide tools for consolidating the aspirational identity, such as goal-setting, resolutions, affirmations, and visualization.

The second pillar, Awareness, includes all the core tools to support you on the path of living from your strengths and becoming your aspirational identity. The four core tools are mindset (shifting negative thoughts), witnessing (letting go of negative thoughts), imagination (creating positive states through your mind), and embodiment (creating positive states through your body). We then explore how these four tools are enhanced by the practice of meditation, the foundation of the Awareness pillar, and cover some meditation techniques that are beneficial for self-confidence.

The third pillar, Action, is all about what you can do differently in your daily life to build and expand your self-confidence. It includes special activities, boosts for quick confidence, and challenges for overcoming your fears. We'll also cover guidelines for improving your skills, recovering from failure, and relating to others from a place of authenticity.

We have dedicated one part of this book to each of these three pillars. These pillars don't have any hard dependencies among them; that is to say, you can go through them in any order and focus on the techniques that feel most promising for your current needs. That said, if you want a more fundamental and permanent self-transformation, then use the tools of the Awareness and Action pillars to support the deep work of the Aspiration pillar. While developing an empowering mindset and consistently taking bold action are beneficial and "good enough" for many purposes—our transformation won't be complete. An underlying sense of impostor syndrome or low self-esteem may still lurk somewhere in there. This challenge is only fully overcome by working at the root of the problem: your identity or self-image.

Identity is the foundation of everything else, and shifting it is how real self-transformation happens. So if you get the Aspiration pillar right, the other two pillars will happen almost automatically, or with little effort. If you ignore this part of the work, you'll have to maintain the other practices consistently for quite a while, until your identity eventually changes as a result of repeated experience. Shifting your identity is the ultimate goal. In this book, it is both the beginning and the end of all our work.

Finally, please keep in mind that implementing any of the practices in this book will require self-discipline. They are all practices of *awareness* and *willpower*, which are the two core elements of self-discipline. If you do the practices only once or twice, you will reap limited benefits.

For deep, long-lasting self-transformation, you will need to maintain a regular practice for some time until it becomes second nature.

Self-discipline is the lens through which I see everything in personal growth. Indeed, transforming yourself is an act of self-discipline—or rather, the result of ongoing acts of self-discipline. If self-discipline is something that comes natural to you, great. If not, then I highly recommend you pay special attention to chapter 18, where I summarize key concepts from my Mindful Self-Discipline framework. That material will be relevant regardless of which self-confidence approach you choose to emphasize.

PART 2

THE ASPIRATION PILLAR

Living Inside Out

5.

Find the Best in You

Everybody is a genius.
But if you judge a fish by its ability to climb a tree,
it will live its whole life believing that it is stupid.

—attributed to Albert Einstein

You often feel tired, not because you've done too much,
but because you've done too little of what sparks a light in you.

—Alexander den Heijer

The one thing that you have that nobody has is you.
Your voice, your mind, your story, your vision.
So write and draw and build and play and dance and live
as only you can.

—Neil Gaiman

When you are in a state of self-confidence, you are focused on *possibility*. You are focused on your strengths, resources, and capacity. By contrast, when you're in a state of self-doubt, you are focused on uncertainty, potential dangers, lacks, and weaknesses. Therefore, the first method for growing self-confidence is learning how to identify and rely on your strengths.

Strengths are potentials for excellence that can be enhanced via awareness and willpower (effort). We all have strengths. But we are not all aware of them. Even fewer of us are actively tapping into our strengths in every area of life. So how do we get started?

There are modalities in coaching that focus almost exclusively on finding and developing people's strengths. This work involves a lot of soul-searching, and it's a process I take many of my clients through. Here, I have shared some of the questions I ask my clients so you can begin identifying your strengths on your own. Be patient about this process, as you might face resistance or find it challenging to gain clarity. For best results, block out an hour on your calendar to actually think them through and write down your discoveries.

- What are some things you can do easily that others seem to struggle with?

- What would people who know you best say is your greatest quality?

- What activities naturally take you to a state of flow?

- What is one thing your friends really admire about you?

- What are three things you most love about yourself?

- What strengths helped you overcome challenging life situations the most?

- What qualities allowed you to get good results in your personal and/or professional life?

- What is unique about you?

- What strengths naturally come from your weaknesses?

- What experiences, background, and values have shaped you?

- What achievements are you most proud of in your life?

Reflect on your answers. What strengths or qualities came up multiple times, even if in different forms? How can you use those strengths to overcome the self-confidence challenges you might be currently facing?

Your core strengths are your personal superpowers. Chances are, simply by becoming more aware of them—by answering the previous questions—you already feel better about yourself. The more you use your strengths and uniqueness in your life, the more confident and capable you will feel. You'll be living more authentically. You'll naturally experience more motivation, resilience, and flow. For example, if you have the strengths of perseverance and patience, then you can be confident in knowing you will stick through any problems that show up until you eventually figure things out. And if building connections is one of your strengths, then you know you can tap into a wealth of resources and support anytime you need them.

You don't need to have the strengths of other people in order to succeed in life. You can rely on the ones you have and go about life in your own unique way, without needing to compare yourself to others and feeling that you are coming short of "the norm." Love the special qualities that make you *you*. Humility might not be the strength of choice in sports, nor creativity in accounting, nor charm in programming. But if that is your strength, then own it. Use it to the maximum. Carve your own path, and show the world a new way to succeed in your chosen activity.

It's true that you can develop any quality or virtue you need. You have that capacity. Yet for the purpose of feeling confident and empowered, owning and leaning on your core, innate strengths are a great start.

LEAN ON YOUR STRENGTHS

It is not enough to have strengths; you need to be *aware* of them. And it's not enough to just be aware of your strengths; you need to *own* them, embody them, and appreciate them.

Are you comfortable owning your strengths? Can you give yourself credit when you work hard, feel proud when you achieve something difficult, and accept genuine compliments? Many people have negative beliefs that prevent them from fully tapping into their strengths. For example, they may downplay their strengths and gifts in fear of being perceived as arrogant. When they do that, they undermine their confidence. Do you fall into this trap from time to time? If so, please remember that it's not arrogant to own your strengths and like who you are. Those who suggest otherwise are those who do not want you to feel your own power—because they are afraid of theirs. Or perhaps they are insecure and want to keep you small.

Another limiting belief regarding strengths happens when you compare yourself with other people and think, *I can't call myself courageous. That person is courageous; compared with them I've got nothing.* Every strength is subjective; what is courageous for one person may not be a display of courage for another. Owning your strengths is about you, not other people. It's not about comparing yourself to some external standard or "perfect example" of a strength, but about finding what things in your life you can rely on as resources.

Lean on your strengths. Don't run away from them. Don't pretend they don't exist. Let them shine through your thoughts, speech, and actions. This is being kind to yourself because it's authentic and empowering. This is also being kind to others because it can inspire them to develop the same strengths in themselves and own the ones they already have.

Your strengths are part of your uniqueness. It is your duty to know them, use them, and walk this earth as a powerful being. The more you focus on your strengths, the more you put your weaknesses in perspective and bypass self-doubt. If you effectively maximize your strengths, your weaknesses will likely become irrelevant.

One way of focusing on your strengths is to choose activities and paths in life that make use of such strengths. In other words: do more of what you are good at. Play a game that you can win.

Another way is to use your strengths as your go-to resource, almost like a mantra. Whenever you are facing a new challenge or feeling low in self-confidence, ask yourself: *How can I use my strength of X, Y, and Z here?* This may not always be the best way to solve a problem, but it's a great starting point.

You feel confident when you play to your strengths and make a difference in the world while using them. It is enjoyable and energizing. So find your *awesome* and live that unapologetically. That's the best way you can live for yourself and for the world.

Sometimes you have a strength in one area of life, but may not know how to transfer that into another area. Maybe that idea has not even crossed your mind. There is an old Japanese story that illustrates this point.

Centuries ago, a master of tea ceremony once crossed paths with a skilled swordsman in Japan. Because of a misunderstanding, the swordsman felt offended by the tea master and challenged him to a life-or-death duel. Japanese culture heavily emphasizes keeping one's honor, so when such a challenge is seriously placed upon you, you have to accept it or be seen as a coward, which is considered worse than death.

Now, the problem was that the tea master knew nothing about sword fighting, and he only had a couple of hours to prepare before the challenge. So he went to see his friend, a samurai, for lessons in swordsmanship. The samurai, seeing the hopelessness of the case, told his friend, "When you meet your opponent, serve him tea."

The tea master understood exactly what that meant. So when he met the swordsman, he held his sword with full presence and gravitas, the same way he would hold a teapot during tea ceremony. Standing like the bronze statue of a war hero, sword in hand, the tea ceremony master was exuding confidence, concentration, and mastery from every pore of his body. The swordsman, realizing he had underestimated his opponent, apologized and called off the fight.

The tea master couldn't fight, but he had some personal strengths that would have made him a formidable warrior—and that also made him look like one. You too have strengths in your life that can be used to face all sorts of challenges. Perhaps you can manage three kids yelling at each other every morning and get them to school on time while still keeping the house in reasonable order. Perhaps you have research skills that enable you to find rare information, connect the dots, and learn everything about your favorite topic on the web. Perhaps you have a great eye for detail when decorating your home or good planning skills for curating the perfect overseas trip.

And you may think that these strengths are confined to those particular areas of life, but that's not the case. Now that you are more aware of your strengths, it's time to ask yourself: What would it mean for you to "serve tea" in the other areas of your life? What strengths are you underutilizing? What domain in your life needs them most?

ACCEPT YOUR WEAKNESSES

Leaning on your strengths makes you feel more confident and empowered, but what about your weaknesses? If you obsess about them, you'll feel like you are never good enough; but if you pretend they don't exist, you might be fooling yourself and limiting your growth. The balanced approach is to *accept* your weaknesses without letting them define you, and then make a wise decision about what is worth working on.

Accepting your weaknesses is a way of freeing your mind from obsessing about them. Whatever you accept, you stop thinking about; it stops bothering you. When you don't accept something, when you can't tolerate it, then you'll keep thinking about it. And a mind that is full of thoughts about one's weaknesses and lacks is not a happy mind—nor a confident one. But does that mean that acceptance is always the best way forward?

No, not always. Sometimes it is worth putting in tremendous effort to overcome a particular weakness. At other times this would be a waste of energy, and this effort would be better invested in other aspects of your growth.

How can you tell the difference? If a particular shortcoming of yours has the capacity to hold you back from living your best life or achieving your goals, or if it causes harm, then it is worth working on it. For example, if you have great organizational skills but poor people skills, you just can't be an effective leader—you'll first need to work on your weakness until you achieve at least a minimum proficiency in that skill. On the other hand, if you can circumvent a challenge by using your strengths, then there is no reason to choose the harder path. If you are a writer with great ideas and vocabulary but terrible command of punctuation, you don't need to work hard in mastering grammar; instead, hire a good editor.

Accepting your weaknesses is not an excuse for psychological laziness. In other words, it's not a reason to think, This is just how I am. I always bluntly say what I think, and expect that everybody needs to swallow that. That would be inconsiderate and entitled, to say the least. If your behavior hurt others or yourself, then saying that it's a shortcoming and that you can accept and love yourself despite it doesn't really help. Don't pretend that you cannot change things that are actually within your power, in the name of self-acceptance, just because you are unwilling to put in the work.

When you decide to work on your shortcomings, aim to do so from a place of wholeness, and not from a place of not-good-enough-ness. That means you are not seeking to improve yourself so that you can feel confident, but because you are committed to growing as a person and excelling at what you do.

Everybody has weaknesses; it is just part of being human. Many people link their sense of self-worth to their shortcomings and experience low self-confidence as a result. Instead, link your self-worth to your strengths and values, and how much you have grown them. A fish will never be able to fly; so it shouldn't measure its self-worth based on its ability to fly. If you are a fish, stop wishing that you could be an eagle and fly high—instead, be an amazing fish! Be the best fish you can be. Embrace your fish nature, and swim far and wide.

You can choose your aspirations and dreams in life. You can choose the game you want to play. You don't need to choose something just because it's easy, but make sure you are playing a game you can win. That way, you can go further with the same amount of effort and enjoy the journey. If you play a game you can never win, there is no way you can be confident in life; you will meet frustration every step of the way. So, how do you know if your answer to "Is this is a game I can win?" comes from insight or from self-doubt? Only wisdom and awareness can help you discern.

Accepting your shortcomings is an act of self-love. It involves seeing yourself as you truly are, and not as you pretend to be. Initially it may require sacrificing some false pride, yet ultimately it makes you feel more comfortable within yourself, which is a requisite to feeling confident. From that point, you can then choose to work on overcoming your shortcomings or decide that they don't matter and that your effort is better spent elsewhere. In any case, you move forward from a place of integrity and self-honesty.

When you own not only your strengths but also your weaknesses, you live with greater self-knowledge and authenticity. You are okay with the fact that people may see your shortcomings, mistakes, and struggles. This makes you more calm, confident, and even likeable. People admire and trust those who are secure enough to be vulnerable.

Exercises

Knowing and owning your strengths is a great way to increase your confidence. When you know yourself and are rooted in your qualities and values, you don't need validation from others to help you believe in yourself. You trust in your abilities, even if others actively doubt and discourage you.

The following exercises can help you solidify the concepts covered in this chapter.

Strengths Acknowledgement. Go through the list of questions at the beginning of this chapter. Reflect on your answers and consolidate a list of five to ten strengths you have. If you struggle with owning these strengths, try turning them into short statements and repeating them in front of a mirror. For example, you could say, "I am enthusiastic and determined" or "I'm a person others can rely on." Do so until you feel you can say it without feeling either discomfort or conceit.

Strengths Use. Brainstorm three new ways you can use each of your core strengths, especially in life domains where you have not yet applied them.

Weaknesses Self-Awareness. Make a list of up to ten of your short-comings. Next to each one of them, write down either "I'll accept it" or "I'll work on it," depending on whether it's worth the effort based on your values and aspirations.

Empowered Experiences. List ten to twenty times in your life when you accomplished something difficult, used your strengths to overcome a challenge, or persevered despite obstacles. It doesn't matter in which area of life those wins happened or how big or small they were. Anything you can find as evidence that you can "make it" is good enough. This will reinforce the awareness of your strengths and give you the feeling that you can do it again.

Imprinting Confidence. Select three of the most powerful experiences you listed in the previous exercise. Go deeper into those experiences, one at a time, and extract the maximum self-confidence you can from them by following these steps. (For a guided meditation version of this exercise, refer to the *Going Deeper* section at the end of the book.)

1. Take your time to visualize the empowered experience in great detail. Remember where you were, the time of day, and the people and circumstances around you. Remember the challenge and how it felt. Make it as real as possible. Feel it as if you were there right now.

2. Remember how you overcame the challenge. Focus on the positive feelings of doing so—maybe energy, empowerment, purpose, or relief. Focus on the positive self-talk you had at that time and how it enabled you to move forward.

3. See if you can remember how the emotions felt in your body. Spend a couple of minutes dwelling on that positive experience. Allow those sensations to expand and take root in you. Where in your body do you feel that state? What is the sensation like?

Identify if it is warm or cool, focused or spread out, shallow or deep, vibrating or still.

4. Visualize the action you took and how that brought a positive resolution to the situation. Celebrate the win inside yourself and let that feeling grow.

Strengths Journaling. Here are some questions to guide you through a daily strength awareness exercise:

- How did I use my strengths today? Feel grateful for those moments.

- Did I misuse or overplay any of my strengths? Become aware of that.

- Which strengths do I want to use more tomorrow? Create an intention.

- On a scale from 1 to 10, how much did I live my strengths today? Assess.

6.

Design the Best You

The greatest sin is to think yourself weak.

—Swami Vivekananda

*A human being always acts and feels and performs
in accordance with what he imagines to be true
about himself and his environment.*

—Maxwell Maltz

Argue for your limitations, and sure enough they're yours.

—Richard Bach

The previous chapter was about finding the best in you as you are now. This chapter dives into the other side of the story: creating who you want to be. First, we talked about self-discovery, and now it's time to focus on *self-design*.

Designing yourself is about having a clear vision of who you want to be. It is about choosing your core values and beliefs. It is tweaking the deepest aspect of your personality: your identity. From here, everything else naturally unfolds.

YOUR IDENTITY, YOUR LIFE

The brain's primary mission is survival. Whenever there are competing projects, interests, or pursuits, the focus on survival will always be its number one priority. You can't fall in love, pursue long-term goals, or create art while there is a tiger running after you.

For survival, it's important that first we save energy, and second that we know how to safely navigate the world around us. Our identity does exactly that. It is a map, a shortcut to effectively navigate life. Our identity tells us who we are, what the world is like, and how we should move in it. It determines how we feel about ourselves, what is safe or dangerous, desirable or undesirable. In this way, it helps us save energy, as we no longer need to constantly figure things out anymore. We can just refer back to our template for life in every circumstance.

Your life is the result of your actions. Behind all your actions are your thoughts and feelings. Behind your thoughts and feelings are your mindset and beliefs. And at the core of your mindset and beliefs is your *identity*. Therefore, your identity determines your life. Any type of self-transformation that is meant to be permanent needs to be a transformation of your identity or self-image; otherwise, it will be like trying to push a boulder uphill. Over time, the identity always wins.

Once your identity is formed, your mind will keep reinforcing it over and over again. That identity will be the lens through which you see the world. This is known as *confirmation bias*: you pay attention to things that confirm your identity and core beliefs and ignore things that don't fit into that model, for you feel that they "cannot be true."

So, in summary, this is the first point to be understood about identity: it is the most powerful force in your life, it is self-perpetuating, and it is the foundation of everything else. It feeds upon itself and upon every event in your life.

The second key point about your identity is this: it is not true. It is also not false. It is a *story*. It is the most important story in your life—the story of you. Yet it's still a story, not a fact, not a truth. This is actually great news because it means you can change it. You can believe another story into existence—just as you have believed your origin story—and take that as the new basis for your life.

It is shocking that in our life the essential element of *identity* gets formed almost accidentally in childhood, influenced by our family and other environmental factors. Then most of us spend the rest of our lives living inside that box. We may decorate the box, give it a different name, and even raise our head to peek outside from time to time—nevertheless, we're still living inside that box.

That box may include the sense of "I don't belong" which makes you feel like a stranger in your own family and an outcast in society; as a result, you fear rejection and are moved toward people-pleasing. It might contain the view that the world is a dangerous place, which leads to anxiety, shyness, and avoidance. Your box may include the sense of "not being good enough," which will push you to work hard your entire life while you secretly feel like an impostor or a failure. Or it could be unhealthy perfectionism, typically as a result of overcritical parents or bullying at school.

Most people live in boxes like these.

Now, here is another option for you: that you dare to dismantle that box. That you have the courage to face the unknown for some time as you watch everything you thought you knew about yourself fall apart. And that you have the inner discipline to create a better box to live in. Your brain won't let you stay without any box for long. We need reference points in order to navigate the objective world, but at least you can now take control of the most important factor in your life: your identity.

Paper essentially has no content, so it will take any ideas that are written on it. Water has no shape, so it will take on the shape of the container it is in. Likewise our consciousness, as our essential being, has no content and no shape; it will display the content and shape that we give it. To stay in the essential nature of consciousness without any box is the path of spiritual liberation; to creatively shape your box to suit your purpose and values is the path of creative living.

Since consciousness can take any shape, in the play of life you can take on any role. This fact, once thoroughly internalized, will likely be the most empowering discovery of your life. The implication is that you can shape yourself according to your will and creative design, rather than just letting it be a consequence of your past conditioning (about which you had no say).

Who you think you are is the result of a lifetime of conditioning. It is not the truth of you. You didn't create your origin story, but you believed in it for years and likely continue feeding it to this day. Now you have the opportunity to change that. This is the ultimate hack in personal development: changing your identity or self-image directly, rather than changing the thoughts and behaviors that spring from it.

Adding a layer of positive thinking or even positive emotions on top of a foundation of "I can't do this" or "I'm not good enough" is hardly sustainable. These mental waves will eventually collapse back into the ocean (your foundation) and leave you exactly where you were before. This is why what you have tried so far hasn't fully worked. With a different foundation, the same affirmations and exercises have a different effect.

Let me give you a simple example. The philosopher Friedrich Nietzsche once said, "What doesn't kill you makes you stronger." Is that really true? Is that helpful? Well, it depends on your identity. If you have the identity of resilience, ownership, and self-belief, then yes, everything you go through in life will make you stronger, wiser, and more resourceful. But if your identity is one of self-doubt and anxiety, then things that hurt you but don't kill you will still break you little by little. The core difference is your identity and the mindset that comes from it.

Whether you believe you can or you can't, you're right.

—Henry Ford

Your identity is a true self-fulfilling prophecy. And the problem is you didn't write it.

It's time to change that.

This chapter and the two that follow will teach you how to create and bring to life the new version of yourself. You will learn how to live from your aspirational identity, rather than your conditioned identity.

SELF-ACCEPTANCE VS. SELF-DESIGN

Grant me the serenity to accept the things I cannot change, courage to change the things I can, and wisdom to know the difference.

—The Serenity Prayer

Before we talk about changing your core programming by redesigning your identity, let us address a common objection, which is, "Shouldn't I just accept myself as I am?"

Self-acceptance is highly valued in the worlds of mindfulness and therapy—and for good reason. It eliminates inner conflict, brings some peace of mind, and liberates your energy for other things. However, self-acceptance is only half of the story. It's an important tool, but it shouldn't be your *only* tool. Just like a hammer is an important tool, but if all you have is a hammer, you'll treat everything as a nail—and not everything is a nail. If you try opening a bottle of tomato sauce with that hammer, I bet you'll never forget this lesson.

Here is a fact that is hard to contest: as a general rule, accepting things makes you less motivated to change them. What are you more motivated to change—a personality trait you can learn how to live with or one that bothers you so much that it becomes unbearable and unacceptable? When one of your traits, habits, or behaviors is unacceptable for you, perhaps because it causes a lot of pain to you or to people you love, you are highly motivated to change it. You will be more focused on making that change, as there is a sense of urgency.

There are things about yourself that you don't need to accept. Actually, with the risk of losing some of my mindfulness friends, I'll go a step further and say: there are things about yourself that you *should not* accept, for it would be unwise to do so. What would you think about someone who thinks, I know I'm aggressive, narcissistic, and selfish, but

I accept and love myself as I am? Likely you'll think it's not a good idea for them to practice self-acceptance in that manner.

Yes, it's possible to accept something and still work to change it, but only if that change doesn't require every drop of your blood and effort. For deeper changes in yourself or your life, only an unbearable pain of dissatisfaction will give you the fuel you need.

> *We change when the pain of changing is smaller*
> *than the pain of remaining the same.*
>
> **—attributed to Tony Robbins**

Accept the things you *cannot change*, such as your fixed physical attributes, your core values, and your past. Accept the things that you *could change* but are not worth it because they are not that important for your aspirations. But don't accept your limitations, flaws, and shortcomings if they are holding you back from living your values or if they are hurting others. Change them. You can change almost everything you don't like about yourself or feel insecure about. And it all starts with how you choose to see yourself.

Find your essence, your truth, your core. Trust it, own it, and love it. Then go and design your identity and your life around it, to bring out the best in you and embody the changes you want to make.

DESIGNING YOUR NEW IDENTITY

Imagine your life is a movie, and you get to design your own character. Who would you choose to be? What would your personality be like? What might be your likes and dislikes, your desires and fears, your aspirations and qualities? What emotions would be moving you? What journeys would you be undertaking?

These questions are not answered in five minutes. Rather, they are the fruit of deep thought and self-awareness. In this chapter we'll go through some exercises to help you develop clarity about who you are and who you want to be. This will be the foundation for you to not only feel confident and act confidently, but to *be* confident at your core.

Designing your new identity is, in a way, about deciding who you want to be without the constraints of your conditioning. It is exercising the ultimate creative power in your life. It is throwing away your old maps of life and meaning and adopting new ones instead. The old maps will take you to the same old places; the new maps will take you to where you want to go.

I say "in a way" because although the choice is an expression of your free will, it doesn't happen in a vacuum. You will tend to craft your new identity in a way that is in alignment with your core values and deepest aspirations—the stuff that makes you *you*. This doesn't mean that your designed identity will only be a rehash of things you are already good at; it may actually contain qualities you perceive to be truly lacking in your life, traits that don't naturally "flow" for you, yet that you deeply long for.

For example, let's say you tend to always put other people's needs before your own. That may be purely an expression of your conditioned identity—you people-please as a way to avoid conflict—or it may be an expression of your core values of generosity, friendliness, and service. If it is the former, you could definitely design your aspirational identity to be more assertive and authentic, if you wish. But if it's a natural expression of your core values, then trying to remove it by designing an identity of individuality and self-reliance will likely not work. It will feel forced, and your energy will not be fully available for that transformation because it's simply not aligned with your values.

Finding your core values and the aspirations that spring from them is beyond the scope of this book; I encourage you to read my book *Mindful Self-Discipline* for those topics. For the work we are doing here, it's enough to understand that the process of designing our identity will happen within the master structure of these deeper elements, whether you are aware of them or not.

Your identity is your personal foundation. Just like a tall building needs a deep foundation, the life you create for yourself will always be determined by the depth of your personal foundation. How do we build this foundation? There is no fixed way to go about it. Perhaps you already know, intuitively, how you'd like to reinvent yourself; or maybe you haven't articulated that yet. In this section you will learn two ways of designing your aspirational identity: a bottom-up approach (Choose Your Symbols) and a top-down approach (Choose Your Power Words).

Exercise 1: Choose Your Symbols

What stories, movies, novels, or TV shows most impacted you growing up? What characters in those stories did you most identify yourself with or want to be like?

These questions are more meaningful than they seem on the surface. It's not about your choice of entertainment genre; it's about identifying the *symbols* or *archetypes* that form your personal mythology. These symbols and archetypes can be a powerful template for your life. They show you how you long to grow and express yourself. They represent the emotions, stories, and aspirations that deeply move you. Each of them is a mode of being with its own "superpowers" (strengths) and "mission" (purpose).

There are different ways to find out what these symbols are for you. Thinking about what fictional characters you identify yourself with is one way. Thinking about your role models in different domains of life is another. You can also think in a more abstract way, by considering which universal archetypes move you, independent of any specific character. The list of archetypes and their qualities is endless, but here are some examples to help you think through this process:

Universal Archetype	Motto	Examples of Qualities
King / Queen	I lead	Leadership, Wisdom, Virtue, Decisiveness
Warrior	I fight	Strength, Purpose, Courage, Resilience
Dreamer / Magician	I create	Vision, Charm, Power, Imagination
Lover	I connect	Aliveness, Trust, Dedication, Art, Joy

Mother	I nourish	Love, Sacrifice, Empathy, Care, Patience
Guide / Mentor	I teach	Wisdom, Perspective, Service, Self-Mastery
Explorer	I explore	Curiosity, Openness, Bravery, Playfulness
Journalist	I inform	Truth, Integrity, Discernment, Independence
Logician / Scientist	I explain	Analysis, Intelligence, Clarity, Persistence
Rebel	I challenge	Self-Reliance, Sharpness, Freedom, Zest

In some traditional cultures, there is the exercise of finding your "spirit animal"—which is a symbol in nature of the characteristics you want to embody in your life. Here are some examples:

Spirit Animal	Examples of Qualities
Ant	Diligence, Cooperation, Loyalty
Bear	Strength, Authority, Understanding
Cat	Independence, Curiosity, Mystery
Dog	Protection, Loyalty, Affection
Frog	Adaptability, Transformation, Sensitivity
Elephant	Strength, Determination, Royalty, Honor
Fox	Cleverness, Skill, Luck, Evasiveness
Lion	Power, Courage, Loyalty, Independence
Horse	Wisdom, Respect, Wild, Service-Oriented
Shark	Drive, Focus, Instinct, Fierce
Dolphin	Joy, Generosity, Friendliness, Intelligence

In the contemplative traditions of the world, also, this technique is widely used. In the Christian mystic tradition, they practice imitating Christ and his virtues. In the Tantric traditions of India and Tibet, practitioners choose a deity from their wide pantheon that represents who they want to "become like." For example, they may meditate on Lakshmi for more abundance, on Hanuman for strength, on Baglamukhi for the power to stop evil, or on the Green Tara for wisdom.

As you can see, there are many ways to find your symbols, and you can go about it in any way that feels right for you.

So this is the first step of the process: choose a "template" for your new identity by identifying the symbols and archetypes that inspire you. If you end up with multiple archetypes, you may notice that there are several overlaps, and often they are all different expressions of the same core desires, emotions, and journeys. At other times, they may express different parts of yourself, some stronger than others.

The second step is to figure out what it is that you value in these symbols/archetypes. Get really clear and specific here. Here are some questions to help you brainstorm this.

- Qualities and strengths. If you love Rocky Balboa films, what exactly do you find most inspiring about him? Is it his work ethic and self-discipline? His perseverance and mental toughness? His determination and self-belief?

- Emotions and desires. If you identify with the archetype of the explorer, why is that? What moves the explorer in you to act? What elements of the explorer's way of being do you want to incorporate into your life? What feelings of the explorer do you find powerful and meaningful?

- Journeys and maps. What are your chosen archetypes trying to achieve? How are they going about it? How do they see the world? How do they navigate danger and opportunities?

- Stories. At their core, how do your archetypes see themselves? How do they feel about themselves? What is their origin story?

Go through this process for each of your symbols or archetypes. I encourage you to write down your answers and be as specific as possible. Conclude this second step by consolidating your insights into a short list of words or sentences. These will then be refined into what I call your "Power Words."

Exercise 2: Choose Your Power Words

Power Words is a concept I use in my coaching to denote a group of three words that have deep meaning for you and can be used as a compass for living. They bring clarity and focus. Instead of having twenty different things to remember, pursue, and practice, you have only three. They are simple and specific, being a single word each, but also rich in meaning.

There are three types of Power Words: the ones focused on your core *strengths*, the ones focused on your core *values*, and the ones defining your *aspirational identity*.

- Strength Power Words are the words that define your core strengths or qualities, as discussed in the previous chapter. These are things you already have and wish to tap into further. You decide on your top three strengths so you can easily remember them and use them more often in your life. Knowing them gives you confidence and power.

- Value Power Words are the essential desires or true longings in your heart. They are the deeper *why* behind the journeys you are on and the goals you pursue. They are a compass for your decisions, showing you what you really care about and what to focus on in your life. You can call it your mission, your dreams, your *dharma*. Knowing them gives you purpose and motivation.

- Aspirational Power Words are the characteristics that you most want to have. They are the new strengths, qualities, feelings, and states you are trying to embody. They are the essence of all your symbols, the summary of who you aspire to be. Just like your strengths, they are also in service of your core values. Knowing them gives you focus and energy.

Your core strengths and core values together are the essence of who you *are*—the DNA of your soul. Your aspirational Power Words are the essence of who you *want to be*. They are what you are practicing. Once a Power Word becomes natural after repeatedly shifting into it for some time, then it moves from the aspirational category to the strengths category.

The previous chapter talked about finding your strengths; finding core values, on the other hand, is beyond the scope of this book. In this next section, we will focus on choosing the Power Words for your new identity. You can get to them by choosing your symbols/archetypes and then finding the elements in them that inspire you most. That is the bottom-up approach we just discussed: starting with the specific and getting to the universal. Another method is the top-down approach, where you choose your Power Words directly by reflecting on the qualities, emotions, and strengths that you long to have. Then you can look for specific examples of them, so you have a more concrete expression to focus on.

Here are some questions to help you identify your aspirational Power Words:

- What qualities do you most admire in others?
- What virtues or strengths would change your life if they were highly developed?

- Think of your most painful experiences in life and the emotions you most dislike feeling. Which words express the opposite, the positive state?

- Think of three experiences in your life when you were at your best. What was going on at that time? What strengths were you expressing?

- What states or emotions feel most magical for you?

Take note of everything you find through this brainstorm. Then look for the overlaps and see if you can define them as a single word—either a noun or an adjective. These words represent qualities that are the key ingredients for you to feel happy with yourself and your life.

If you have chosen many words, then classify them into groups and try to find the word that best represents the group as a whole, being the deeper meaning behind them all. The goal is to narrow your list down to three such words.

Here are some examples of aspirational Power Word trios from my coaching clients:

- Calm, Confident, Creative

- Trusting, Accepting, Joyful

- Competent, Playful, Courageous

- Clear, Empowered, Disciplined

- Carefree, Confident, Loving

- Self-Trust, Fearlessness, Contentment

- Resilient, Selfless, Disciplined

- Wisdom, Integrity, Power

- Originality, Purpose, Abundance

Every aspirational Power Word is a *practice*, a commitment. If you can meaningfully answer the question "What does it mean to practice X right now?" then X is an aspirational Power Word. Otherwise, it might be a core value instead. If you want to brainstorm Power Word ideas, you can search the web for "list of strengths" or "virtues list" for ideas, then use a thesaurus to find the best variant of each.

It's worth mentioning that one person's aspirational word might be another person's strength word or even core value. It's also entirely possible that ten different people have ten different interpretations for a single word. The important thing, then, is not the dictionary definition of a word, but the subjective experiences it evokes in you.

If you struggle with self-confidence, then likely *confident* will be one of your aspirational Power Words. Or you could choose a related word, such as *strong, powerful, indomitable, unstoppable, whole,* or *courageous.* Check in with your head, heart, and gut to find which word feels right for you. Then choose an archetype or symbol that contains the type of self-confidence you want to have while still being aligned with other aspects of your ideal self. You might need to find a different symbol for each Power Word.

If you want to really geek out on the Power Words, you can have different trios of strengths-values-aspirations for different areas of your life. Although it's not necessary, you may find that this flexibility is useful, especially in the domains of relationships and work. These secondary trios may have big overlaps with your main trios, or they may be considerably different.

For example, my Power Words for core strengths are: discipline-perseverance-insight; and for core values, space-power-exploration. For my work with Mindful Self-Discipline, the core strengths are depth-completeness-clarity, and the core values are purpose-power-peace. As a father, my core strengths are playfulness-wisdom-support, and my core values are freedom-empowerment-love.

Different Trios in Different Areas of Life

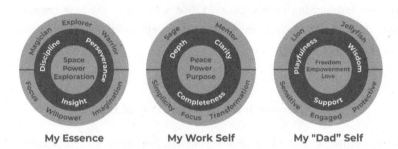

| My Essence | My Work Self | My "Dad" Self |

As you can see, there are obvious overlaps: clarity and wisdom are an expression of insight; exploration is a form of purpose; and the word *power* shows up in all three. Still it was a helpful exercise to find distinct words for different areas of my life, as there were some new elements to be found—such as love, support, and peace.

Each Power Word will likely contain the meaning of secondary words within it. In my case, if we take the Power Word "perseverance" (one of my core strengths), it contains optimism, commitment, patience, resilience, dedication, and purpose. Any of these words could be chosen as the main one of this group, and that choice is personal. For me, "perseverance" was the strongest and most encompassing one in the bunch.

You can also play with the idea of adding a qualifying word before your Power Word to make it more alive or more focused for you. Sometimes doing so will change the original meaning or clarify the specific aspect of it that you desire. For example, "contentment" pure and simple feels different from "deep contentment," "selfless contentment," "blissful contentment," or "peaceful contentment." Using the theme of this book as an example, "wise confidence" points to a different experience and approach than "unstoppable confidence" would.

You don't need to obsess about finding the perfect Power Words in any of the trios. They will evolve over time as you grow in self-awareness.

For now I suggest you spend some time thinking about this, then move forward with the words you find. It's okay if you only have one Power Word for now, or if your words change as a result of doing this work. Remember that the *aspirational* Power Words are the most fluid. They simply represent what you are focused on becoming right now and how you are redesigning your identity. Once it becomes the new normal, it will then change to accommodate other self-transformation journeys you may want to embark on.

Exercise 3: Choose Your Way of Life

In designing a new identity for yourself, you may find it helpful to include not only universal archetypes and Power Words but also specific words that define your key roles, core habits, and lifestyle choices. Some examples include athlete, vegan, health-nut, entrepreneur, artist, Christian, *bon vivant*, existentialist, lifelong learner, writer, meditator, spiritual seeker, hacker, storyteller, pet lover, stylish, productivity geek, punk, or traditionalist. Each of these is a more concrete element of one's identity, and they come "pre-packed" with certain core habits, philosophies of life, and lifestyle choices.

This extra layer is not essential for the purpose of developing self-confidence, but since you are redesigning your identity anyway, you might want to include it as a means of helping you anchor certain positive habits and strengths into your new self-image.

Accessing Your Template

Once you define the essence of your new identity via the methods above, the next step is to learn how to embody and express that template. You may feel that the words or symbols you have chosen are far away from who you are today. It may feel impossible for you to *be* that person right now. In reality, this is only the case because the old identity feels familiar, and thus "true," while the new identity feels foreign.

The way forward is to remember your essence, the contentless and shapeless nature of consciousness, which can take on any identity. In practical terms, this means you have the inherent potential to be whatever you conceive of yourself.

Whatever strengths, aspirations, journeys, and stories inspire you in your symbols, know that you have these same qualities within yourself—at least in seed form. That is why they resonated with you in the first place. Something inside of you wants to grow into that new self and needs your help. Your symbols and Power Words are a template, a shortcut to access something that *already exists* inside of you.

Find that experience, that strength, that mode of being within you. If you trust that it's there, you can find it; if you doubt it, it will elude you. So trust that it *is* there, even though you might not have proof of it yet. Consciousness is the storehouse of all possibilities, so it definitely has what you are looking for. You might have already had an experience of expressing that template, so you can tap into that memory and expand on it (you'll learn how in chapter 12). If you haven't had such an experience yet, you can use your imagination to conjure up that mode of being (see chapter 11).

For this to work, you'll need to

- be open to the possibility of operating from a new identity;

- imagine it as already real and believe it into reality repeatedly;

- have the intention of synchronizing your consciousness to that "frequency";

- confirm it day by day through your self-talk and actions.

I call this process, *living inside out*. It is an inner discipline that requires patience and perseverance, yet makes everything else possible.

LIVING INSIDE OUT

There are two ways to live.

One way is looking for feedback from your environment and the people around you in order to form your self-image. Your focal point is external, and you seek validation there. The opinions of others impact you deeply, and your past experiences of success and failure determine your current sense of self-worth. Your identity is a question mark: *Is it okay for me to feel like this? Can I be this way? Do I have the right to believe in myself?* I call this *living outside in.*

The other way is *deciding* who you are, then constantly affirming that decision through your thoughts, words, and actions. It is holding on to the image and vision you have of yourself with full determination yet full humility, regardless of feedback to the contrary. Your focal point is internal, and you need no external validation. What you think of yourself is more important than what others think of you. You are led by your values and aspirations, not by the opinions of others. Your identity is an exclamation mark: *This is who I am!* And your daily life is an expression of that commitment. I call this *living inside out.*

When you are living inside out, you are your own center of gravity; when you are living outside in, you gravitate toward other people's. "Outside in" is conditioning; "inside out" is freedom. Living outside in is bondage; living inside out is creative.

To shift from your conditioned identity to your aspirational identity, you need to live inside out. That process is the dual effort of consistently affirming the new identity and letting go of the old identity. The next two chapters will explain these fundamental practices, then the Awareness and Action pillars will provide further tools to support the process.

A person wanting to fly high in a hot air balloon, into new lands, will need to have fuel for the journey, and they'll also need to drop the weight that holds them to the old ground. Only then can they overcome its gravity. Likewise, your old identity has a strong gravity. It's what feels most natural and perhaps even most true. It's what your environment is supporting you to be. To break free from it, you will need to develop a stronger force in a different direction, and also let go of what is keeping you chained to the old way of thinking. This is "letting go of the old identity."

Through the exercises in this chapter, you have designed your new identity based on what you already know about yourself (your values and strengths) and based on what you want (your aspirations). Now it's time to *live* it. You do that by choosing to see the world from those new lenses, thinking from a new set of beliefs, and acting from new assumptions and motivations. That internal shift needs to happen daily, repeatedly, until the new identity gains strong momentum. This is "affirming the new identity."

Whenever you make that internal shift, the way you think and feel in the moment will change. You remember your symbol, archetypes, or Power Words, realign with them internally, and live from that space. This means thinking and behaving as the person you want to be, not as your past conditioned you to be. In other words, you make choices based on your aspirational identity, choices that affirm your higher self. This is freedom and power. This is the ultimate expression of what Carol Dweck calls a *growth mindset*.

In every moment you have the choice to think and act from your conditioned self or from your designed self. Every time you choose the conditioned self, that's a step back, a "-1" in your life; every time you choose your designed self, that's a step forward, a "+1." Every action and every thought either moves you one step away or one step closer. Becoming aware of this, and living accordingly, is the inner discipline of self-transformation.

Conditioned Identity
Your past creates your future

-1 No Discipline

You

+1 Self-Discipline

Aspirational Identity
Your aspiration creates your future

Act as who you want to be. Think from that foundation. Remember your new identity daily. Move toward it constantly. Affirm it with patience, and believe in it relentlessly. Gradually it will become the new you. It *has* to, for consciousness is fluid and shaped by thought.

This is not about repressing thoughts of self-doubt by pushing a layer of positive affirmations on top. Instead, it is becoming a new person through your conscious design—a person who doesn't have that self-doubt problem anymore. In a way, you overcome that obstacle by embodying the self that has never had that challenge in the first place.

For example, if your aspirational identity contains the Power Words *confident* and *resilient*, you shift into that mode of being by believing yourself to be full of confidence and resilience already and acting from that belief. Decide that that is who you are, and confirm it via your actions. Tap into that feeling by rekindling a past memory of when you felt that way or using your imagination to identify yourself with a symbol or archetype that has those qualities.

Something inside of you *knows* what it's like to be strong and resilient in a given situation. Something inside of you knows what it's like to face challenges with the courage of a lion. Something inside of you knows what it would feel like to walk into a room as if you were Bruce Wayne or Katniss Everdeen.

You just don't express those qualities because you have a limiting belief that you are not like that, or that you don't have the right to be that way, or that you have to naturally feel like that to act in such a manner. Adopting an aspirational identity that is confident and resilient at its core removes these inner obstacles, giving you permission to be that way here and now. It's a shortcut.

Practicing this inner shift is simple, but not easy. It might take some time for this approach to fully bear fruit for you. If you feel that you don't exactly know how to do it yet, don't worry—it will get clearer as you progress through the book. Every chapter will explore a different aspect of this technique.

Living inside out is a process, a journey; but, more than anything else, it is a *decision*. It's a commitment to yourself. You don't need anybody's permission for it. You don't need to look into your past to check if it's possible or not—your past won't help you.

Once you find that template inside yourself, then it's about holding on to it steadfastly and merging yourself with it. You decide that, from this moment on, This is who I am. Conceive that your higher self has those qualities, those feelings, that template, and that now it's time to own it all and begin to express it. Water the seeds of that new way of being through repetitive affirmations, belief, and actions, until they germinate.

Take a moment now to make a commitment to yourself to *live inside out*. Whenever you catch yourself looking for feedback or validation about who you are or who you can be, remember to shift to your designed identity and adopt it as your new reality.

Be an exclamation mark, not a question mark.

MEDITATION: CONSOLIDATE YOUR RESOLUTION

In the Yoga tradition, there is a lying-down meditation technique called *Yoga Nidra*. Most people think it is only a practice for relaxation and sleep; however, one of the main purposes of this technique is to plant a resolution deep inside your subconscious mind. Hence, this practice is relevant for our process. Although a thorough explanation of the Yoga Nidra technique is beyond the scope of this book, there are a few steps to keep in mind as you design your resolution.

The first step is to craft a short, clear resolution out of your aspirational identity. In the meditation world, the term for resolution is the Sanskrit word *sankalpa*. A *sankalpa*, or resolution, is like a deep commitment or a vow—not a petition or a request. It is a lasting change you would like to create, a determination to transform yourself or your life in a particular way.

Your resolution should be expressed in simple words, in the present tense, and in an affirmative manner. So, for example, instead of "I won't feel insecure in social interactions anymore," you articulate it as, "I am confident and courageous in all my interactions."

For example, if your aspirational Power Words are calm-confident-wise, your self-transformation resolution could be something like:

- I feel calm and confident every day.

- My true self is confident and wise, and I live from my true self.

- I am always calm, confident, and wise.

- I face every challenge with confidence and wisdom.

- My wisdom deepens every day.

- My calm is unshakable.

You would choose one of these sentences—or craft your own—and use it for Yoga Nidra and affirmation practice (to be covered in chapter 8). Once you choose a resolution, it is best to always express it in the same words and to stick to that resolution until it is fulfilled.

So how do you practice Yoga Nidra? There are multiple steps, and this meditation is almost always a guided practice. You can seek a guided audio from a teacher you trust or follow the free version I have created here: MindfulSelfDiscipline.com/wise-confidence-bonuses.

A daily practice of Yoga Nidra is a great support in consolidating your aspirations. It is the formal side of the practice. The informal side is constantly shifting from the old to the new multiple times a day, tapping into your symbols and Power Words at every opportunity. Together, they support the ongoing process of letting go of the conditioned identity and nurturing the aspirational identity.

7.

Break Free from Your Conditioned Identity

Within you right now is the power
to do things you never dreamed possible.
And this power becomes available to you
just as soon as you can change your beliefs.

—Maxwell Maltz, author of Psycho-Cybernetics

Don't look back—forward, infinite energy,
infinite enthusiasm, infinite daring, and infinite patience—
then alone can great deeds be accomplished.

—Swami Vivekananda

No one can make you feel inferior
without your consent.

—Eleanor Roosevelt

The quicker you are willing to let go of your old self-image (conditioned identity), the quicker you'll be able to embody the new one (aspirational identity). And although the path ahead is clear, it's not necessarily easy.

Your old identity, with all its limiting beliefs and negative emotional patterns, has tremendous momentum to it. You have believed it, affirmed it, and even fiercely protected it for many years. While you are in the process of shifting to your aspirational identity, the conditioned identity will continue to exist for some time, and you'll need to learn how to deal with this past momentum.

The main challenge in this process is that the prospect of dismantling your conditioned identity feels scary. Your current identity may be causing you suffering, sure, but it still feels like "you"—which means that letting go of it can feel like death. During this transition period, a big fear of the unknown can come up. Something inside of you may be resisting this change, doubting whether it's really a good idea. It's like the caterpillar who wants to be a butterfly (aspirational identity) but is afraid of letting go of its cocoon (conditioned identity), for it feels like death.

To overcome that, you need one of three things: courage, faith, or unbearable pain.

- Courage is a positive response in the face of fear. It recognizes the fear yet resolutely moves forward because it sees on the other side something more valuable than the fear. Courage is the willingness to confront pain and uncertainty without turning back.

- Faith is your ability to trust the process and suspend all doubts. It is a sense of certainty that arises within you beyond the realm of reason. It is this conviction that going through this journey is the right thing to do, even if you can't prove it yet.

- Unbearable pain removes all your options. If your conditioned life is so painful that you've got nothing to lose, you'll try anything.

This is the first and last test in this journey: Are you willing to let go of the security of the known—your conditioned identity—and *temporarily* inhabit the limbo state of the unknown?

The past is certain, albeit painful; the future is uncertain, and you don't (yet) have the complete confidence to move forward. So you will need to trust this process. The more you become aware of how much you *need* this transformation, the more likely it is for courage and trust to arise in you. If you want to reach for the skies, you must be willing to let go of the security of the ground—at least for the time being, until you find higher ground.

The seed needs to die into the earth in order to become a mighty tree. The caterpillar needs to "die" as a caterpillar in order to emerge as a butterfly. In the rites of passage of many tribes, the boy needs to die as a boy so he can be reborn as a man.

You can only be reborn as your new self after you die as your old self. So the courage of letting go and the faith that there is something better on the other side are key elements to this process. And these are not things you either have or you don't—they are qualities you learn to cultivate.

GET READY FOR CHANGE

Let's go through some exercises that will help you be more courageous, motivated, and ready for the journey. You will find these helpful if you are experiencing resistance letting go of your conditioned identity.

Facing the Worst

Make a list of all the resistances you have to adopting your aspirational identity. List all the fears, all the ways you think "this is not right" or "this is not going to work," all the bad things you think may happen. Try to be as specific as possible. Then go through each of those fears and ask yourself:

- How likely is this to happen? Attribute a percentage to it.

- From one to ten, how bad would it be if it does happen?

- If it happens, what can I do to fix it, recover from it, or at least minimize the pain?

- If it happens, is a blessing hidden somewhere in there?

- What are the benefits of getting through this fear and completing the journey?

- Am I happy to let this fear stop me from experiencing those benefits?

The awareness and clarity that comes from this exercise is often enough to efface, or at least manage, your fears and doubts.

In the past, when I was faced with the fear of the unknown in this journey, with the fear of "disappearing," I found strength in the following thought: *If I don't like it, I can always go back. The old identity will always be there, waiting for me.* This idea is related to the third question above. It worked for me, and you may find it helpful too.

The conditioned identity is the power of the default, so gravitating back to it is always an easy option. There is fear when you go on a path of no return, but there should be no fear when you can easily get back to the *status quo*.

Black and White Clarity

Clarity brings focus and motivation—and with that, power. If you feel that you are not so motivated to go through the journey of self-transformation, it is likely because you are not fully clear about what's really at stake here.

The simplest way to look at it is this: there are two possible versions of your future self, and you get to choose which one you want to feed, moment after moment. With every choice, you are either taking a step toward your aspirational identity, or you are confirming your conditioned identity. There is no confusion about it: it is either a "+1" or a "-1."

I call this *Black and White Clarity.* Thinking in this manner helps you gain full awareness and full focus. It's important to see the sharp contrast between these two future selves; otherwise, we tend to hide in the middle, in the grey area. You fall in the grey area because it takes less effort. It is less risky and less threatening. But your transformation, then, is only mild; you are kind of motivated, kind of confident, kind of happy, and kind of successful.

The grey area is the easy way out. It is you giving a chance for your conditioned self to feel satisfied with just getting a *little bit* better, instead of you becoming your aspirational self in all its glory. You are decorating your box instead of dismantling it. To be all that you can be and go as far as you can go, you need all the fuel you can get. And this comes from understanding the huge contrast between the two possible versions of your life.

In one version, you've stayed attached to your conditioned identity (living by default). In the other version, you've become your aspirational identity (living by design). In one version, you stay stuck in the life template handed down to you by your parents and society; in the other, you create and live your own template, your own symbol.

Which future do you want? Which person do you want to be? Do you want to be a product of your environment, or do you want to be a *creator*?

If you become your designed identity—which has more confidence and more of the other qualities you desire—your life will be different. Take some minutes to reflect on the following questions and get clear on exactly *how* different it would be.

- Step 1. If ten years from now, you are still carrying the same mental and emotional patterns, the same habits and limiting beliefs, what would you have or experience in each area of your life? Fill in the column on the left.

- Step 2. Now think of your designed identity with its Power Words. Imagine that you have that new way of thinking, that new self-image, and those new strengths. If *that* is who you are, what would you have or experience in the different areas of your life? Fill in the column on the right.

- Step 3. Compare the two columns. Let it sink in how *different* these two possibilities are for you. Allow this insight and the feelings that come with it to fully motivate you for the journey.

	Conditioned Identity	Designed Identity
Health		
Career		
Finances		
Love Life		
Fun		
Social Life		
Mission		
Spirituality		

What is possible for your aspirational identity is not possible for your conditioned identity. Realize that letting go of your past, of your conditioned self, is a very small price to pay for the benefits you will get. Turn your fear into excitement as you step into the world of possibility.

If I were to wish for anything,
I should not wish for wealth and power,
but for the passionate sense of the potential;
for the eye which, ever young and ardent, sees the possible.
Pleasure disappoints, possibility never.
And what wine is so sparkling, so fragrant,
and so intoxicating, as possibility!

—Søren Kierkegaard

Rituals of Transition

Being ready to face fear and having clarity on the possibility of a new way of being are powerful ways to prepare you to let go of the conditioned identity, so you can be your new confident self. Now let's shift gears to a more external exercise: creating a ritual of transition.

Most major transitions in life—such as graduations, marriages, birthdays, moving homes, product launches, retirement, and funerals—are either marked with a ritual or are a type of ritual in themselves. There are also rituals for transferring power to a new president, honoring a war hero, or getting initiated into a spiritual tradition. A ritual is a set of steps or actions that mark an event as significant and help us process a transition. Something important has happened, and now something has changed. We are not in the same place as before. We are not the same person as before.

Rituals are a helpful tool for making a change in life, which always involves letting go of the old state and welcoming the new state. That is how having a ritual for the transition of your identity—from the conditioned one to the aspirational one—can help. This ritual can be designed by you and include any actions or steps you find meaningful.

Here are some ideas to consider for your ritual of transition:

- Burning an object that symbolizes your old self
- Renewing your wardrobe
- Deleting old files, emails, and photos
- Getting a meaningful tattoo
- Redecorating your office or bedroom
- Starting a new class
- Moving to a new home, city, or country
- Writing a letter to yourself
- Having a difficult conversation and closure with someone

- Changing jobs, or even careers

- Ending certain relationships

- Going on a long retreat

- Creating a radical change in your daily routine
  or lifestyle

Making changes to your environment and external life can be helpful when you want to reinvent yourself. Otherwise, the old environments and relationships may continue to invisibly pull you back, triggering negative emotions and reminding you of the old, unconfident version of yourself. Through awareness and willpower, it is possible to overcome these influences, yet it all gets much easier if you have a change in environment.

The general goal is to be around people and environments that affirm your new identity and to take a break or get some distance from people and environments that pull you back into your old way of being. A ritual might be the tool you need to consolidate that transition deep into your psyche.

CULTIVATE OWNERSHIP[1]

Blaming others is a means of experiencing some emotional comfort while still staying inside your old box, by pretending that it's not your fault and you have no control. Blaming *yourself* means taking full control, but in an unbalanced way; it keeps your attention locked into fixing the box. Both attitudes, although seemingly opposite, have the same effect: they keep you busy with the life inside the old box—either by seeking justice or by seeking self-punishment.

Whenever you are blaming others or blaming yourself, you are actually reinforcing your old identity—your old way of seeing things, feeling things, and navigating the world. You are trying to fix your life from the perspective of the conditioned identity (your past). You are using your old maps, but hoping to get to new places.

It's hard to be confident that you can overcome life challenges if a big part of your energy is spent blaming *others* for those challenges. It's also hard to feel confident if you are constantly beating yourself up for past mistakes.

When you move from blaming others to taking ownership, and from blaming yourself to *designing* yourself, then your energy is freed from trying to fix the past and is made available for re-creating your present and future.

In a way, you could argue that your conditioned identity is not your fault. It was the hand of cards you were dealt. Yet thinking like that can lead to either passive resignation or resentment, neither of which are helpful. The truth is, whatever your conditioned identity is and whatever contributed to its creation, you have the power, *here and now*, to let go of your old way of being and reinvent yourself.

Ownership means taking full responsibility for your existence and for where you are in life—your successes, your failures, your goals, your healing, and your growth. It is focusing on what you can control and accepting what you cannot. Ownership is power, because you can never change anything that you don't take responsibility for.

The opposite of ownership is victimization. Believing you're a victim keeps you stuck, because when you are in victim mode, you feel that there is nothing you can do to change things. You feel that you have no control, no power. You can only blame, be miserable, and play the "poor me" card, hoping that others will come and help you—or at least show some compassion. These things might feel good in the moment, but they don't really help you transform.

Ownership is not "victim blaming." The wrong and hurtful things people did are their responsibility, and they need to pay for them. Yet your well-being is ultimately your own responsibility. In this scenario, ownership is about taking responsibility for *your* life, *your* emotions, and *your* healing process. It means that you are not waiting for an apology before you can move on. It means you are not expecting life to always be fair. You are not waiting for anything outside of you; instead, you are taking charge and moving forward by yourself.

If lack of ownership makes you blame others, an excessive sense of ownership makes you blame yourself. This is a problem too, because instead of using your energy to create and inhabit your new identity, you are focusing it on feeling bad about your past mistakes.

Ownership presupposes a balanced understanding of what is under your control and what isn't. If you think all is under your control (unbalanced responsibility) or if you think nothing is under your control (unbalanced acceptance), you fall into distortions of thinking known as *control fallacy* in cognitive behavioral therapy (CBT). What we need is the mature understanding that most things are not under our control, but how we respond to them is. The stories we tell ourselves, the choices we make, and the self-talk we cultivate—that is. In sum, we cannot control the outcome, but we can control where we put our attention and our efforts.

Taking ownership is about believing that you are the architect of your destiny. Circumstances may not be favorable and people may do you wrong, but at the end of the day, you have the power to decide what it all means and choose your next steps. You don't even need to forgive anyone; you just need to let go and focus on being the best version of yourself. You can pair this, of course, with learning to take better care of yourself by setting boundaries in relationships (see chapter 17).

Letting go is a power you always have. However wrong the other person was, however unfair the situation was, you *always* have the power to learn something from it and let it go. You always have the power to outgrow it. This is an important point to drive home; otherwise, all your energy will get consumed in blaming others and victimizing yourself—and from this point of view, letting go of the old identity is not possible.

You can only tap into your innate ability to let go once you have the courage to stop looking for things to blame in others and are ready to do what *you* can to move on. Instead of trying to understand who put you in your original box and why, you are focused on building yourself a better one, as per your design.

Real maturity begins when you finally realize that nobody is coming to rescue you. It is only when you accept 100 percent of the responsibility for who you are that you are ready to let go of the past, design your confident self, and begin living in harmony with it.

Take full responsibility for who you are right now—and for who you can become. Refuse to allow your past to determine your future. Make a plan to improve what you can improve, but never allow your insecurities to be an excuse for you to doubt yourself and show up half-heartedly. When life calls you in for a fight, when challenge knocks at your door, deal with it with full courage, focus, and self-belief. Assume you will succeed *and* work hard for it.

EMBRACE THE PROCESS

When you turn off a fan, it will continue spinning for a while due to the force of its past momentum. There is no longer any new energy making it move, yet it continues to move. The same happens when you go through this process of shifting from the conditioned identity to the aspirational identity. Even if you are super-aware and disciplined and don't give any new power to the old patterns, they will continue to show up for some time. That is completely normal, so don't let it discourage you.

When the old self-talk comes back saying that you can't do this, that you are not good enough, or that you will fail like you have failed in the past—look at it with compassion and say, "Thank you for trying to protect me, but I don't need this type of protection anymore. I've got this." Then immediately affirm your new identity by repeating your resolution (*sankalpa*). For example: "I believe in myself no matter what, I can achieve anything," or "There is great power within me, and I'm committed to manifesting it," or "I'm always confident, [Power Word], and [Power Word]."

Don't just say these affirmations mechanically. Feel them. Intend them. Believe them into existence. Then enjoy the feeling that comes when you move toward your new self.

This process of thanking the old and reaffirming the new is a simple way of slowly releasing the grip of the conditioned identity. In the Awareness Pillar you will learn other tools that help you overcome your conditioning, such as:

- questioning, deconstructing, and replacing negative thoughts (chapter 9)

- observing the old thoughts from the perspective of a detached witness (chapter 10)

- releasing negative emotions with the ROAR Method (chapter 10)

- snoozing unhelpful thoughts with the Not Now technique (chapter 10)

- using imagination to shift your past or dissolve negative thoughts (chapter 11)

All of these are different ways of shifting or breaking free from the old patterns. Every time you shift like that, you are taking one step closer to your ideal self. In Mindful Self-Discipline, we call this "getting a +1." This shifting is an ongoing process, and our goal is simply to accumulate as many "+1s" as possible, until the old fan stops spinning.

Your aspirational identity is full of confidence and the other qualities you seek. But your conditioned identity has strong momentum to it and will constantly pull you back, even after you completely stop feeding it. Persevere through that phase, and embrace the process. Use whichever tools you need to constantly break free from the limiting patterns of your conditioned identity until your consciousness fully releases that old way of being.

We've covered how to release the old. In the next chapter we'll talk about the other side of the process: how to affirm the new.

8.

Align with Your Aspirational Identity

The biggest commitment you must keep
is your commitment to yourself.

—Neale Donald Walsch

Believe in yourself. You are braver than you think,
more talented than you know, and capable of more than you imagine.

—Roy T. Bennett

The foundation of self-confidence, the basis of boldness and self-assertion,
is a deep inner trust, based on living a life of perfect integrity,
and disciplining yourself to live consistent
with your highest values in every situation.

—Brian Tracy

At this point you have defined your aspirational identity—your confident self—and have begun the process of breaking free from the conditioned identity. So what's next? To actively live from your new self! To constantly remember it, feel it, and act from that point of view. To create and pursue goals that affirm that new way of being.

It all starts with a deep commitment to your values. Your aspirational Power Words (see chapter 6) are not a wish list for who you want to be, but a *commitment*. They are a resolution. They start as a vision, but need to be confirmed through action. It is the practice of self-discipline, which I define as "your ability to live life in harmony with your values."

This means that if your aspirational identity includes confidence, then you need to tune in to the mode of confidence—inherent in consciousness—and *be* confident. You choose to pursue goals you would naturally pursue if you had that confidence. You choose, say, and do things your old self would dread, but that feel natural to your new self. In other words, you act as if you are already your empowered self. You confirm your new self-image by consistently taking action based on it.

You may ask, "Is this the same as 'fake it till you make it?'" You could say that it's the more enlightened version of that concept. The difference is that you are not faking it, but *creating* it. Those who call it "faking" don't understand the mechanics of it nor the fluid nature of identity. Knowing that you are not confident and merely pretending you are for the social benefits of it is faking. *Deciding* that your true self is confident, then doing your best to act in alignment with it, is creating. There is a subtle yet profound difference.

Whenever you act in alignment with your values and with the vision you have for yourself, you feel great. You feel empowered and authentic. That already boosts your confidence and self-respect. Besides, living in integrity with your ideals is not easy, and whenever you do something that is not easy, your sense of self-confidence increases.

Don't expect your Power Words to magically manifest into your life simply because you have chosen them. You need to actively tap into your Power Words throughout the day. Manifest them, through your willpower and resolution, by incorporating them into the way you think, the things you say, and the choices you make. Use them as your compass for living.

Men become builders, for instance, by building, and lyre-players by
playing the lyre. Similarly, then, we become just by doing just things,
moderate by doing moderate things, brave by doing brave things.

—Aristotle

Act like the person you want to be. Display the qualities that your
aspirational identity has. Bring your future into the present until there
is no difference between the two. This is the path forward. It is not
complicated, but it does require cultivating some self-discipline and
perseverance (see chapters 18 and 20).

Consistently ask yourself, What would my ideal self do here? Then
see what happens. It doesn't mean you will always act in perfect alignment with your aspirational identity, but it will certainly move the
needle in that direction. Do this for long enough, and that will become
your new default. Eventually you'll get to the point where you will stay
authentic to your aspirational identity consistently and naturally. Your
vision will have become your reality.

THE DAILY ALIGNMENT PRACTICE

Character has to be established through a thousand stumbles.

—Swami Vivekananda

The practice of becoming your aspirational identity is the practice of
shifting from the old to the new multiple times each day. For that purpose, begin each day by purposefully connecting yourself with your ideal.
The best time to do this is in the morning, before the busyness starts and
definitely before you go online and expose your mind to the world of
outside in living. Make it a habit to connect with yourself and with your
vision before you allow any other influences into your day.

I call this the *Daily Alignment Practice*. It can take anywhere from
two to thirty minutes, depending on how much time you have and how

deep you want to go. It is composed of three steps: remembrance, affirmation, and visualization.

Part 1: Remembrance

The first step, remembrance, is simply reconnecting with your aspirational identity. You can do that by reading your Power Words, thinking about your symbols/archetypes, and optionally reviewing the Black and White Clarity exercise so you can reconnect to why your aspiration matters. All of this lights up and reinforces the new neural network in your brain that's associated with your designed identity. You'll then use affirmations and visualization to further consolidate it.

Part 2: Affirmation

I realize that the dominating thoughts of my mind
will eventually reproduce themselves in outward, physical action,
and gradually transform themselves into physical reality;
therefore, I will concentrate my thoughts for thirty minutes daily,
upon the task of thinking of the person I intend to become,
thereby creating in my mind a clear mental picture.

—Napoleon Hill

In chapter 6 you created a *sankalpa*, which is a strong resolution that encapsulates your aspirational identity. You can use this as an affirmation that empowers you to be your best self. For example: "I am full of courage, confidence, and energy."

The first thing to understand is that an affirmation is not about describing reality, but creating it. It is choosing your future self and bringing it to the present, repeatedly, until that gap eventually disappears. Never mind that for a while you will get feedback to the contrary from your environment, and perhaps even from your inner experience. It's the old fan still spinning. Resolutely persevere and focus on what you are creating, not on feedback. Remember, this journey is about living inside out, not outside in. Over time, your aspiration will bend reality in your favor.

The second thing is that, for an affirmation to be effective, its practice should not be mechanical. If you are just going through the motions, repeating it merely on a verbal or intellectual level, you'll get very little from it. For best results, you need to repeat it with concentration, willpower, faith, and feeling. These four keywords are extremely important.

- Concentration: While repeating your affirmation, focus all your attention on it. Just like in meditation practice, let go of distractions and keep your awareness with your object—in this case, the sentence. Stay with it wholeheartedly, as if it's the only thing in the universe.

- Willpower: Have a strong intention that your affirmation is true and *must* be true. Remember, this is a *resolution*, which is an intention with great force. Just like you need to tighten your muscles to hold yourself to a hanging bar, tighten the muscles of the mind to hold steadfast to the thought-current that you are creating, and thus energize it.

- Faith: You have to believe it. If part of you is saying you are courageous, but another part of you is going against that same thought, doubting it and bringing reasons to the contrary, then you are divided. You have weakened that thought-current. Instead, have faith in it. Believe it into reality. Faith is a *choice* and has no requirements. If you choose to believe it, then you do. It is the "act as if it's real" part.

- Feeling: If your affirmation says that you are full of confidence, then make sure to create the feeling of confidence within you. Don't wait for it to magically appear—*produce* it, based on the power of your imagination or based on previous experiences of confidence. The created feeling is then enhanced by the first three elements.

An effective affirmation practice creates a blueprint via imagination and consolidates it into reality through the power of the mind. *Feeling* is an expression of imagination, which directly produces the state that it conceives of. *Concentration, willpower,* and *faith* are expressions of the power of the mind (*manas shakti*)—they breathe life into that which is being created.

The Elements of Affirmation Practice

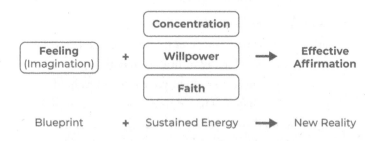

So this is your practice: repeat your affirmation ten times every morning, with concentration, willpower, faith, and feeling. This will take about two minutes. If you also meditate, do your affirmation practice right after your meditation, when the mind is naturally calmer and more focused.

If you have any secondary affirmations that you also find empowering, you can do them after your main one. These secondary aspirations can be a bit more flexible in their form and can serve any purpose you need. Here are some ideas that are relevant for building confidence:

- "I *can* do this. I *must* do this. I *will* do this." (This is a useful mantra by Swami Rama that helps you when contemplating a goal or challenge you're facing.)

- "My aspirations are more important than my fears. My goals are more important than my doubts."

- "I have the capacity to become who I want to be. I will overcome whatever challenge comes my way."

- "I have in me all the strength and resources I need to fulfill my aspirations."

Whenever you need to make the shift from the conditioned identity to the aspirational identity during your day, remember your affirmation. Repeat it out loud if possible, or whisper it to yourself. And always do so with concentration, willpower, faith, and feeling. Then close the day by repeating your affirmation ten more times before going to bed.

Part 3: Visualization

The third step of the *Daily Alignment Practice* is visualization. This is not about visualizing the effortless achievement of the end result, so popular these days. It is, rather, about visualizing the *process*. You see yourself going through your daily life, facing a challenge, then responding from your aspirational identity instead of the conditioned identity. This trains the self-confidence response, or whichever of your new strengths are relevant to that challenge.

This technique is called POWER Visualization, and it comes from my Mindful Self-Discipline framework. It can be used for cultivating any new behavior. Here are the steps:

1. Preparation. Sit or lie down comfortably. Close your eyes. Get to a calm state of relaxation by using your favorite meditation technique or simply by focusing on your breathing for a few moments.

2. Obstacle. Visualize yourself working toward one of your goals or ideals, then facing an obstacle on your path. Visualize it with as much detail as possible. Feel how it feels at that moment—the fear, self-doubt, and

avoidance that may come. Notice how these feelings take you directly to your conditioned self.

3. Willpower. See yourself pausing, becoming aware of the situation, and intentionally making the effort to shift to your aspirational identity. Visualize yourself remembering the tools you have learned in this book and using your willpower to apply them.

4. Energy. Experience the heightened energy that comes as a result of tapping into your ideal self. Feel how empowering and enlivening this shift feels. Really take it in.

5. Result. Visualize yourself overcoming that obstacle and moving forward, living from the space of your aspirational identity. Enjoy the feeling of confidence that comes from experiencing that you have the resources to overcome any challenges that may come up. Develop total certainty that change and success are possible for you, by seeing it within your mind.

If you'd like to follow the guided meditation version of this process, you can check out the information on the Mindful Self-Discipline program at the end of this book.

BIG ASPIRATIONS, REALISTIC GOALS, BABY STEPS

"There is within every organism an inborn drive toward the complete fulfillment of its inherent possibilities," said the influential psychologist Carl Rogers. I call these possibilities our *aspirations*. They are an expression of our core values and deepest desires. They are the only things that will truly fulfill us. Some of us are in touch with what they are; others don't yet have that clarity.

Yet knowing your aspirations is different from living them. For many people, there is a disconnect. What is it for you? What is preventing you from expressing your full potential and fulfilling the possibilities of your nature? It is likely a lack of self-confidence, because when you are living with confidence, you feel comfortable adopting bolder goals. You believe in yourself enough to dream bigger and take meaningful risks.

A powerful way to affirm your aspirational identity, then, is to allow yourself to dream big. That's what you would do if you had more confidence, right? Live aligned with your higher self by embracing and consistently pursuing the aspirations that your higher self has the strength to pursue. Decide what is true, purposeful, and valuable for you—before you think about what is possible. Get excited by the possibilities before you let the practicalities bog you down. When you are thus energized, then look at the challenges ahead with a spirit of confidence, courage, and optimism. This makes all the difference.

SMART Goals[1]

Once you have clear dreams and aspirations in life, the next step is to translate them into specific goals that help you move forward. Aspirations are lifelong desires or commitments, while goals are short-term projects that help you advance your aspirations. Setting clear goals is essential because without them you won't feel very confident that you can make progress toward your aspirations.

It's not enough to just set any goals; you need to set *effective* goals. If your goals are unclear, unrealistic, too big, or too broad, you will have a hard time making progress on them. This can then demoralize you, demotivate you, and make you doubt yourself.

You need goals that feel realistic and doable—goals that help you build more self-confidence because they allow you to experience progress early and often. This builds up a sense of success and self-efficacy. A great framework for this is SMART goals, which teaches us to set goals that are *Specific, Measurable, Achievable, Relevant,* and *Time-Bound.*

Specific means that the goal is concrete enough that you know what success looks like. "I want to be healthy and full of energy" is an aspiration, and it's not specific. You can't know when you have achieved it. A specific goal for that aspiration might be, "To sleep at least seven to eight hours every night so I don't need caffeine to function during the day."

Measurable means that the success is quantifiable, so you can track your progress. There may be a single variable you are measuring (e.g., money saved, pounds lost, hours practiced, people contacted); or, for more complex goals, you'll need to break them down into milestones or phases. Goals that are more subjective in nature (e.g., "Feel more confident at work") need to get a numerical dimension to them so they become measurable (e.g., "Take my confidence at work from a four to a seven out of ten").

Achievable means that your goal is realistic and attainable for you. You need to feel like you can actually do it; otherwise, it will be hard to keep yourself motivated. Think of the steps, attitudes, skills, and resources you need to make it a reality. If the goal is not achievable, either get the resources you need to make it achievable or set a different goal.

Relevant, in the context of my work, means that the goal is aligned with your core values and aspirations, and it is challenging enough to keep you engaged in the process.

Time-bound means the goal has a realistic deadline. If you don't have a deadline, you may end up procrastinating forever; and if your deadline is not realistic, you're setting yourself up for failure, which may hurt your confidence.

Think of some of the goals you have that you are not taking action on. Rewrite them based on the SMART goals framework and create a clear action plan for each of them. Then check in with yourself and ask, *Do I now feel more confident that I can achieve it? Do I feel more energized to pursue it?*

When you become clear about your values and aspirations and then set effective goals, you begin to tap into deeper resources within yourself. Your brain is charged by a higher current and produces more light. If you truly commit to your goals, the journey you have now set yourself on will *demand* that you be the best version of yourself; otherwise, you won't achieve them. This is a great opportunity for you to exercise the confidence of your aspirational identity. Just like muscles grow by exercising them, confidence grows by exercising it, and we do that by taking on meaningful yet achievable challenges and taking consistent baby steps toward them.

Baby Steps

When the challenge in front of us feels too big for us to tackle, we tend to shrink and shy away. We doubt ourselves, and that kills our motivation. To prevent this from happening, make sure that you break down your larger goals into clear baby steps. A baby step is an action that makes you feel "I can do this." It doesn't feel difficult or overwhelming. There is no self-doubt about it. There is no reason to procrastinate or make up an excuse not to do it. It is clear, specific, and small. You do it, then you feel good—because now you have positive momentum. With every baby step taken, your confidence strengthens. And little by little, these tiny steps compound to huge results.

So, this is the formula: big aspirations, SMART goals, and clear baby steps. Then the journey of achieving your goals becomes a way of expressing your new self-confidence and also a way of exercising it.

When you try to do too much (too many goals) or expect too much of yourself (unrealistic goals), you set yourself up for failure. This, in turn, can break your confidence. Reverse that pattern by making it easy for you to take action and succeed. As you get some successes under your belt, your sense of confidence will definitely grow. Action creates feeling.

It doesn't matter how small your next step is, so don't feel bad about going "too basic." The only thing that matters, especially in the beginning, is that you are simply taking a step forward. And if you don't know what the next step is with your goals, then figuring out the next step *is* the next step. Get help with that if needed.

When you do experience some success, marinate in it. Stay with the positive feeling for thirty seconds longer than you naturally would. In most cases that's all you need to make sure the little win registers. This helps you create a buffer against self-doubt.

SHIFTING WITH THE PAW METHOD[2]

The key to expressing your aspirational identity in daily life is the constant practice of *shifting*. We have mentioned it in the previous chapters, and now it is time to go through the how-to.

Shifting from your conditioned identity to your aspirational identity requires effort. In this sense, it is an exercise of *willpower* and self-mastery. This exercise can take many shapes, such as repeating an affirmation, visualizing something, cultivating an empowering mindset, getting in touch with your strengths, or taking positive action.

The thing is, you cannot use your willpower without awareness, and you cannot be aware without the ability to pause and slow down. If you are living on autopilot, you'll act by default, not by design. In other words, you'll express your conditioning, not your vision.

Therefore, you need to *pause*, then be *aware*, then apply your *willpower*. I call this the PAW Method. Let's compare the PAW Method to driving toward a destination:

- *Pause* is slowing down your car when approaching an intersection.

- *Awareness* is looking at your map, checking where you are, and seeing what the path is to your destination.

- *Willpower* is taking the right path, even if it's a steep hill.

In applying the PAW Method to our daily life, pausing means taking a couple of deep breaths to interrupt the automatic flow of the conditioned self. It is slowing things down so you can see what is going on and potentially make a change.

The ability to pause is one of the main superpowers that comes from a consistent meditation practice; it gives you space, clarity, presence, and groundedness. When you pause, you feel more in control, and thus more confident. When you don't pause, you are just following your conditioning, as triggered by the environment, and that reinforces the old self.

Simply by practicing meditation daily you will already experience more *pause* in your life. You can enhance this process by remembering to deliberately pause several times during your day. To do that, you'll need to set reminders for pausing and reconnecting. It could be an alarm on your phone, a quote pasted on your wall, an object you wear, or really anything that works for you. You can also try using the phone wallpaper images I have created for this purpose. They are available for free download at MindfulSelfDiscipline.com/wise-confidence-bonuses.

Then we come to awareness, which is about knowing what is going on both in you and around you. Has something just triggered you to react from the conditioned identity? If so, what was it? See how the triggered *reaction* is a "-1" in your life, as it is taking you a step away from who you want to be. Then remember your aspirational identity, with its symbols and Power Words. Identify what you can do to shift to that mode of being, and instead get a "+1" by affirming your ideal with a conscious *response*.

Finally, willpower is about making a deliberate effort to shift to your new self. This shifting can happen in many ways, depending on the needs of the moment. Thus, the willpower step is extremely versatile. Making use of any of the techniques in this book to shift to confidence in the moment is an expression of willpower. It could be as simple as repeating your affirmation with strong focus and intention and tuning into that feeling, or it could be applying one of the tools from the Awareness or Action pillars.

Once you have shifted, you then act from that new state. This completes the process.

PAW Method

Conditioned Identity	Conditioned Identity	Conditioned Identity / Aspirational Identity	Aspirational Identity
Before PAW	PAUSE	AWARENESS	WILLPOWER

The PAW Method is the way we align ourselves to our aspirational identity again and again. It is a practice that can be done anytime, anywhere. Aim to practice PAW at least three times throughout your day.

SUMMARY

The Daily Alignment Practice is the foundational work for living from your aspirational identity, so we start each day with it. Then we have the macro practice of shifting to your aspirational identity by embracing your deepest aspirations, setting SMART goals for them, and taking consistent action toward them while embodying the confidence of your new self. Finally, the micro practice is to be constantly aware of when you are drifting back into your conditioned identity and to shift then and there with the PAW Method.

With the skills learned in this chapter and the last one—how to let go of the old identity and manage its mental and emotional momentum—you now know all you need to know about how to transition from your current self to your ideal self. This is not only the core of the self-confidence journey, but of *any* self-transformation journey.

Here is the summary of this process:

Know who you want to be.

Affirm it daily.

Shift to it constantly.

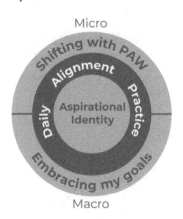

Live based on it.

And let go of everything else.

The rest of this book is a collection of tools to help you practice this new way of life. It's good to *learn* all of these tools, but you don't need to practice them all. Focusing on one or two is much better. Remember, these tools are all different ways of achieving the same thing: moving from the conditioned identity to the aspirational identity.

It's all about living inside out.

PART 3

THE AWARENESS PILLAR

Mastering the Core Tools

9.

Mindset: Shift Your Self-Talk

What we see depends mainly on what we look for.

—John Lubbock

Men are disturbed not by things,
but by the views which they take of them.

—Epictetus

It's not about what happens to you
but what happens in you.

—Mooji

We now enter the second pillar of the Wise Confidence framework, Awareness. In this part of the book, we will cover two approaches for dealing with negative states, two approaches for creating positive states, and the practice of meditation, which boosts all four approaches. This first chapter is all about self-talk, attitudes, and mindset, inspired by the lessons from personal development literature and cognitive-behavioral therapy (CBT).

Let's start by defining some terms.

Our mind is a collection of *thoughts*, most of which are repetitive. The way we tend to think about things, interpret things, and react to things is what is known as an *attitude*. It is basically a cluster of thoughts that give meaning to other thoughts and determine how we relate to them. Thinking you are always right is an attitude (arrogance), as is thinking that other people are often trying to abuse you (victimhood), or thinking you can easily learn whatever you don't know (can-do attitude). If the thought pattern is about how you relate to yourself, then we call it your *self-talk*. Finally, the collection of your attitudes, or mental patterns, is what is known as your *mindset*.

Your life experience is determined by your mindset. Whether you are happy or not, successful or not, empowered or not—it all depends on your mindset. It all depends on the stories you tell yourself. Stories are the engine of meaning, emotion, and decision-making in our lives.

Events, in themselves, don't have any intrinsic meaning. For example, there is nothing in the universe you can point to and say, "This is a failure." Things just happen. Everything is as it is. But our brain attributes meaning to events to fit things into our "map of existence" so that we can navigate the environment, survive, and procreate. Ah, the plan of Mother Nature!

Let's say you are walking and see a friend on the other side of the street. You wave, but he doesn't wave back. You could think any of the following:

- *That's so rude! Why does everybody treat me like this?*

- *He's ignoring me on purpose. I knew he never really liked me!*

- *Did I hurt him in any way, so he is cross with me?*

- *He must not have seen me.*

- *Maybe he is so busy in his head that he didn't recognize me.*

The truth is you don't know what really happened. But your brain doesn't like the unknown, so it wants to interpret the event and create meaning around it. This tendency is perfectly normal, but it doesn't always unfold itself in a way that is helpful or accurate. And it doesn't always feed our sense of confidence.

If you get ten people to share their interpretation of the same event, you'll get ten different stories, ten different ways the same event could be internalized. Each of these interpretations leads to different ways of feeling and reacting to the event. The same event that is internalized as a trauma for one person might not even register as important for another.

Losing your house might be interpreted as a disaster, or it could be the push you needed to make some changes in your life. Your partner breaking up with you might mean you'll end up alone for the rest of your life, or it could simply mean that you were not a good fit for one another. Getting rejected at a job interview might be seen as proof that you'll never make it or as a sign that you need to work on your interviewing skills. One of these interpretations makes you feel depressed; the other, motivated and focused.

The way you talk to yourself matters. A lot. Your self-talk is an expression of your underlying identity, and it's also constantly reinforcing that identity. Your life is not made of events and facts, but of stories. How you feel, what you do, what you pursue—it all depends on the stories you are telling yourself.

Are your stories serving you? Are they creating strengths or weaknesses? Are they helping you fulfill your core values, or are they holding you back?

The good news is your thoughts are not truths. They are just opinions. At a very subtle level, they are *choices*. Your mind suggests a possible interpretation for an event, but you have the choice to believe it or not. That is a core power we all have, yet only a few of us are consciously exercising it.

In this chapter you will learn how to identify disempowering thought patterns, deconstruct them, and instead tell yourself a better story. With this you can change from a self-talk of fear and self-doubt to one of wise confidence.

COGNITIVE DISTORTIONS

Here are some of the most common "thinking errors," as defined by the literature on Cognitive-Behavioral Therapy. They can all be contributing to low self-confidence, so it is important to be aware of them.

Filtering is when you ignore or discount the positive and focus solely on the negative. In this type of thinking, you dwell on the painful or undesirable aspects of a situation and ignore the ways that it could be a blessing. Some ways to balance this tendency include practicing gratitude, shifting your perspective, celebrating your wins, and cultivating optimism.

Making assumptions is a pattern that is hard to escape. It is the brain exercising its creative power to fill in the unknown. The previous example of one's friend not waving back illustrates this point. One way of making assumptions is overgeneralizing, which is taking a few instances of an event as evidence for a broad conclusion. For example, you fail three times at something and then conclude that you will never be good at it. Another form of making assumptions is jumping to conclusions, which happens when you feel sure about your point of view even without any real evidence. For example, when you are convinced that something bad will happen or that people are thinking ill of you when you can't really know.

The way to counter making assumptions, in all of its forms, is to become aware of it and look upon your own assumptions and conclusions with open-mindedness and humility. Hearing others' points of view might also bring in a different perspective. Above all, we need to become comfortable with accepting uncertainty.

All-or-nothing thinking is seeing things in absolute terms: a person, thing, or event is either all good or all bad, either all true or all false. Either you are the best designer in the company, or you "suck"; either you get something 100 percent right, or you are a failure. This type of perfectionism destroys your confidence because you are setting unrealistic standards for yourself and believe that you don't have the right to feel confident unless you meet them.

If your core programming is to interpret mistakes as personal failures, then you will avoid trying new things and being bold in life because it feels risky. As a result, you never give yourself the chance to accomplish difficult things and develop the confidence that comes from doing so. The way to counter this cognitive distortion is to ask yourself specific questions that help you see the nuances and realize all the other possibilities that lie in between the extremes.

Shoulding is another way we can cause suffering to ourselves. It's when you set inflexible standards for yourself, and if you don't meet them, you feel guilt, shame, or a sense that you are not good enough. Some people can use should statements to keep themselves focused and motivated, but for most people it leads to negative feelings that can show up as avoidance, procrastination, or giving up.

Here is where I see things a bit differently than many therapists. "Shoulding" is not always bad—in fact, believing that would itself be an expression of *all-or-nothing* thinking! Having an inner critic is not bad. Being a perfectionist and having high standards for yourself is not necessarily bad either. The question is, is this voice empowering you to be better, or is it simply beating you to the ground? Is the intention of this voice to help you grow, or is it to confirm a low self-worth identity? If you believe that using "shoulds" and "musts" can help you stay positive, motivated, and focused, just make sure that the underlying standards are aligned with your true values and are not borrowed from someone else.

The way to overcome the negative type of shoulding is to realize that your standard is likely arbitrary. It's a choice, and one that you can stop making if it's not serving you. Make sure to bring some self-love into the mix and *live inside out* from your higher self. If needed, rephrase the thought in lighter terms—for example by replacing "should" with "could."

Catastrophizing is when you expect the worst to happen or when you believe that what has happened is worse than it actually is. This makes you exaggerate your mistakes, project failure, and live life under the shadow of anxiety and fear. You make a mountain out of a molehill. Small negativities are seen as a big disaster. It's a form of overgeneralization. You counter this by looking for exceptions, gaining a different perspective, and staying grounded in the facts.

Blaming is also a cognitive distortion, and it was addressed when we talked about ownership in chapter 7. Blaming yourself for things you can't control damages your self-confidence, and blaming others for how you feel makes you feel disempowered and not in control of your life, thus diminishing your self-confidence as well.

As you can see from all these cognitive distortions, our mind creates its own subjective reality, and it's not always a happy one or an empowered one. These negative thought patterns could make you feel bad about your appearance, capabilities, personality, or place in life. This may then lead you to doubt yourself, have unreasonable fear, focus on the worst, and feel discouraged from taking action. In other words, these cognitive distortions undermine the key components of self-confidence: self-belief, courage, optimism, integrity, and willpower.

These patterns are made worse by comparing ourselves to unrealistic portrayals of other people's lives on social media and also by our projections of what others might be thinking about us. Needless to say, this keeps you in the cycle of low self-confidence. In truth, other people don't think about you as much as you imagine because they are too busy thinking about themselves. In any case, their thoughts about you are *their* stories, not yours. Your only concern should be striving to live in harmony with your deeper values and your aspirational identity—in other words, living inside out.

Simply becoming aware of these tendencies can help you realize that much of your self-criticism is ill-advised, much of your fear is just speculation, and much of your suffering is needless. These ways of thinking are just *stories*. If they are neither true nor helpful, then change them!

Before closing this section, I invite you to integrate this knowledge by doing a negative self-talk inventory.

- Step 1: Take inventory of all the limiting beliefs that are damaging your self-confidence. Take note of all the ways you limit yourself or talk yourself down. Include the favorite sentences of your inner critic.

- Step 2: Next to each negative thought, write down which cognitive distortion is at play. There could be more than one.

- Step 3: What can you tell yourself when you catch that type of thought pattern going on? Write a short sentence that will help you shift back to a more accurate, or at least more helpful, way of thinking.

DECONSTRUCT AND REPLACE

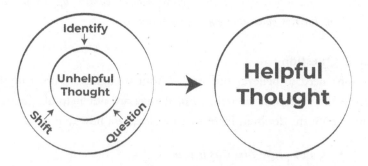

This is the step-by-step method I teach people to help them deal with cognitive distortions and negative thoughts. This involves dialoguing with the thoughts and working with them on their own level.

Step 1: Identify

Shifting your self-talk takes cognitive effort and self-regulation. It is, thus, an act of willpower, and as we saw in the PAW Method (chapter 8), before willpower we need *pause* and *awareness*.

So as soon as you notice you are engaging in negative self-talk, the first step is to stop for a moment and interrupt it. This is *pausing*. Then become aware that there is a thinking error, and identify which one it is. This is *awareness*. If there are negative feelings or unpleasant sensations associated with it, which is often the case, become aware of them too. The goal here is just to acknowledge, not suppress.

If you want to enhance your awareness of these patterns—which is useful, especially in the beginning—you could write down the thoughts that are arising. This helps you objectify your self-talk and gain some distance from it, so you don't get lost in it. Some people like to keep a self-talk journal for this purpose so they can gain greater clarity about their thought patterns. If you go for that approach, then whenever you log your inner dialogue, also take note of your context: where you are, the time of day, who you are with, your energy level, or any other relevant factor.

Another way of increasing awareness, and also of gaining some space in relation to that pattern, is to label the voice or story. For example, you could say, *Ms. Anxiety is here; Oh, the scared boy is coming up; I'm catastrophizing;* or *The not-good-enough voice is speaking.*

Step 2: Question

You don't need to believe your stories. Your thoughts are not true just because they are your thoughts. So, if they are not helpful, question them. Doubt the doubter! Here are some ideas on how to do that:

- Can I prove that this is true?
- Is this thought accurate, or could it be an exaggeration?
- What evidence do I have to support this conclusion?
- If I had to argue for the opposite, what would I say?
- What facts might I be overlooking, ignoring, or discounting?
- In what ways might I be wrong?
- Have I ever been wrong about something like this before?
- Have things ever turned out fine before, despite similar anxieties?

- Would everyone I know interpret this the same way?

- Is this thought helpful, or is it holding me back?

You don't need to go through all of these questions; sometimes just one or two are all you need. And you can also use any other questions you find powerful. The point is to gather evidence to deconstruct your current limiting beliefs.

Step 3: Shift

At this stage, the negative thought has already lost some of its power because you have identified and questioned it. The third and last step is to shift into something more empowering.

How can you reframe your thinking and replace the unhelpful thoughts? Here are some ideas.

- Shift to a more accurate and positive version of the initial thought. For example, you could go from *I never succeed at XYZ* to *So far I have not yet succeeded at XYZ, but I feel that I'm getting better. I'll try again.*

- Introduce a new perspective. For example, you could say, *I'm not nervous, I'm excited!*

- Shift to the flip side of this negative belief. For example, go from *I can't do this* to *I am resourceful. I can do whatever I set my mind to.*

- Use a sentence that reminds you of one of your core strengths: *I am resilient and creative! I'll be able to cope with whatever happens.*

- Try to find the positive in the negative: *Is there anything here I can be grateful for?* or *How is this a blessing in disguise?*

- Bring to mind your main affirmation (see chapter 8), and thus remind yourself of your aspirational identity. Repeat it with concentration, willpower, faith, and feeling.

Write down at least three alternative thoughts that are more empowering, positive, or true. Focus on each of these thoughts for at least thirty seconds, to allow them to really sink in.

Replace the negative with the positive, the disempowering with the empowering, the old identity with the new identity—repeatedly. Replace focusing on your weaknesses and lacks with focusing on your strengths and resources. Replace focusing on what could go wrong with focusing on the rewards of your goal.

There are many ways to shift. Use whatever works for you. Just know that you'll need to do this consistently for some time, until the old thoughts lose momentum and the new thoughts take root. Make a firm determination to replace your self-limiting beliefs with your new beliefs whenever they come, there and then. Do this every day, and one day you will wake up and not even remember that self-doubt was once a problem. At that point, your old identity, with all its limiting patterns, will feel foreign to you.

MINDSETS FOR NAVIGATING ADVERSITY

Every negative event contains within it
the seed of an equal or greater benefit.

—Napoleon Hill

The soul is like a mirror.
If you are irritated by every rub
how will you ever shine?

—Rumi

When you are experiencing adversity or failure, the way you talk to yourself can make or break your self-confidence for years to come. So it is extremely important to know how to navigate these challenges and turn danger into opportunity.

Is failure really proof that you are not good enough, or is it an opportunity for you to learn and grow? Is adversity here to break you or to make you stronger? Will it be a breakdown or a breakthrough? Your choice. You can find evidence for your limitations, or you can find evidence for your capacity. The way you choose to see it will determine how you live and how far you go.

Nothing in your life is really a failure if you learn from it, if you use it to discover something new about yourself, or if you use it to develop new strength. So know that your failures don't define you. Know that every setback is an opportunity to learn and take a new step. When life hits you unexpectedly, reconnect to your *why*, your core values, your aspirations. Let them energize you. The pain of disappointment will go, but your goals will stay.

Your perception of how well you are handling a difficult situation can either reinforce your confidence or dismantle it. You can't really control the adversities that come to you, but you can control how you respond to them and the stories you tell yourself about how well you're managing them. If you feel that you are putting in good effort, trying things out, and tapping into resources you didn't even know you had—you'll feel confident, strong, and proud. On the other hand, if you see yourself shrinking, breaking, escaping, giving up—that will put you in a thought-loop of low self-confidence.

Exercise

To learn more about your mindset around failure and adversity, try the following exercise.

1. For the next ten days, take note of any events that diminish your sense of confidence.

2. Write down how you interpreted each event and the attitudes you brought in.

3. Using the Identify-Question-Shift method, decide how you can better internalize those experiences. Make a strong decision to shift to that new way of thinking, and hold on to it firmly until it takes root.

POSITIVE MINDSETS TO CULTIVATE

So far we have talked about shifting the negative thoughts and unhelpful attitudes that may come up. Now let's talk about the other side of the story: cultivating positive attitudes. This will improve your mindset and serve as a buffer against unhelpful thoughts.

Focus on Possibility

When you focus on problems, you tend to get discouraged, weighed down, and stressed. When you focus on possibilities, you are more likely to be resourceful, optimistic, and dynamic. It is, therefore, a good attitude to assume that there is always a solution to whatever you are struggling with. Actually, there are likely *many* possible solutions. Start with that mindset, with that belief, and let it guide your thinking. You will see that instead of blaming and complaining, you take positive action.

Some people are avid complainers; they find a problem for every solution. "Yes, but . . ." is their motto. An empowered individual is different; they believe there is a solution for every problem, a way forward for every challenge. "What's the solution? What should I try next?" is their formula. "I can't" turns into "How can I?"

This takes us back to the topic of ownership. When you focus on what you cannot change, you disempower yourself. You weaken your willpower, motivation, and confidence. Continue down that path for long enough, and soon you'll get to a point where you feel that nothing you do matters, that *you* don't matter. Instead, reconnect with your strengths and values. Remember your past successes and your resources, then analyze the problem from that energized state. List the possible solutions, choose one to try, and take a baby step forward. Do the best you can, and accept the results. Then learn from it and try again.

Run an Experiment

Having an experimental mindset allows you to try more things in life. It removes the barriers to action and diminishes the costs of failure. When you are just "trying something out," failing at it doesn't hurt your confidence—it was just an experiment that didn't work out as expected.

If there is something you want to do but you are not doing it because you lack confidence, see if you can tap into the experimental mindset and be playful about it. In this way of seeing things, you are not overly concerned with the results. You want things to go a certain way, but you are okay if they don't. This makes you naturally more carefree and daring.

Be Kind to Yourself

Observe your self-talk when you are being hard on yourself. Would you say those things to anybody else in your life? Probably not. Yet you say them to yourself because there is a deep-rooted pattern of self-criticism in your conditioned identity.

Being kind to yourself is an expression of self-love. It is speaking to yourself with the kindness and care you would show a loved one, or at the very least the respect and encouragement you would show a friend. Not beating yourself up for your mistakes and failures is an important part of being confident. As the self-love advocate Whitney Thore used to say, "You cannot hate yourself into a version that you love."

Use the Identify-Question-Shift method as a framework to practice being kind to yourself. The third step, Shift, can be either shifting your self-talk to something more uplifting and loving—like something you would say to a friend in a similar situation—or doing acts of kindness toward yourself. As with everything, this is a *practice*, something that feels difficult in the beginning and natural after many repetitions.

Have Realistic Expectations

When you strongly hold on to certain expectations of success and things don't go as planned, the easiest thing to do is doubt yourself or your goal. Depending on the case, you could even fall into a depressive mood or end up abandoning that goal altogether.

There are two ways to avoid this challenge. One is to have an iron will and unshakable determination so that you can stomach the pains and bounce back no matter what. The other, gentler way is to be wiser about your expectations and hold them more lightly.

For that purpose, avoid what is known as "false hope syndrome," which is when you expect things to happen easily, the path to be smooth, and success to come quickly. If that is your attitude, you may lose confidence when life doesn't go the way you expected. Instead, adjust your expectations regarding the length of the journey and the challenges you'll encounter. Anticipate that things will likely be harder than you expect, and you will be better prepared for the journey ahead.

Also, avoid unfair comparisons. Comparison can bring doubts about your ability and your path. Imagine that you're a beginner artist looking at someone's masterpiece and thinking, I'll never be able to paint like that. Maybe I'm not cut out for this. Or imagine you are an entrepreneur and you think, I'm not progressing quickly enough. I'll never be like Steve Jobs. Are these fair comparisons? No. Never compare your *process* with somebody else's *end result*. You don't need to be better than they are; you just need to be the best version of yourself.

Some days, though, you just have to accept that nothing will work. No technique, no shift, no meditation, no trick. You will likely have those days. Maybe you are just exhausted and need a break. Maybe the stars are not aligning. It doesn't matter. The good news is, those days will pass. Don't lose heart—just keep moving forward, gently but resolutely. You'll be all right.

FINAL NOTES

Shifting negative self-talk to positive thinking and developing empowering attitudes are both great ways to create more self-confidence. If these practices are serving the larger work of shifting to your designed identity, which is confident at its core, even better.

The goal with the practices in this chapter is not to have zero self-criticism and unrealistic optimism; that would be dangerous, as it could lead to arrogance and self-delusion. It's not about never criticizing yourself, or never considering how things can go wrong. A self-confidence that relies on these conditions is brittle.

It is not about shallow positivity and feel-good, but growth and empowerment. For that purpose, you do need to know how to shift away from unhelpful thoughts that just hold you back for no good reason. But you also need to know how to self-reflect and be critical about your actions, the difference being that this comes from a place of self-love instead of self-criticism. This means that if you choose to be strict with yourself, it's because that push is aligned with your deeper values. It's done with the intention of growing and uplifting yourself—not of bashing yourself.

The process of shifting by questioning thoughts, replacing them with the positive, and cultivating helpful attitudes is a powerful tool, but not a solution to everything. When you experience a sudden and intense rush of emotion, just playing at the cognitive level is likely not going to cut it. Likewise if the thought currents are relentless and overwhelming. In these cases, the tools described in the next few chapters, coupled with the aspirational identity work, will be a better bet.

10.

Witnessing: Zoom Out and Observe

*It is the mark of an educated mind
to be able to entertain a thought without accepting it.*

—**Aristotle**

*Your goal is not to battle with the mind,
But to witness the mind.*

—**Swami Muktananda**

*When I dare to be powerful,
to use my strength in the service of my vision,
then it becomes less important whether I am afraid.*

—**Audre Lorde**

I magine that your mind is telling you, *Don't talk to that person. It will
be embarrassing.* You could question this thought, realize that it is a
cognitive distortion, and replace it with a different thought, such as, *I*

am sure it will be okay. He looks nice and kind. I have no reason to believe that it will be a bad experience. And even if it is, I can handle it. That is the approach you learned in the previous chapter.

Another approach is to just be aware that this thought is there, without believing it, and then go and do what you wanted to do in the first place. This is the awareness-based approach of witnessing.

Witnessing is very different from dialoguing with thoughts and actively shifting them. It's simply about remaining as the awareness that *knows* thoughts. It is recognizing the thoughts arising in your mind and letting them all be as they are without "touching" them. And by *thought*, in this chapter, I mean any type of mental phenomena, which also includes memories, emotions, beliefs, triggers, and impulses.

This may all sound abstract to you right now, but please hang on. By the end of this chapter you will know exactly how to use this technique in your daily life. It is subtle, but not complicated.

In a way, witnessing takes much less energy than the approaches that involve engaging with the thoughts. You can use it to deal with any type of negative thought pattern. Witnessing won't change the thought patterns, but it will make them lose their power, thus giving you back the freedom to act based on your goals and values.

When should you use one or the other? Here is my rule of thumb: if you are dealing with a recurring thought pattern that you have never effectively challenged before, then use the *shifting* approach from chapter 9. However, if you have already challenged and shifted that particular thought repeatedly and are convinced of the new thought but the old one keeps coming up out of habit, then you can just witness it. Also, if your thoughts move too fast, or are too confusing, or too loaded with emotion, then witnessing may be easier than shifting, especially if you are trained in meditation. In any case, if one approach proves better for you than the other, adopt what works.

In the world of spirituality, this approach is known as mindfulness in Buddhism (*sati* in Pali) or witnessing in the Hindu traditions (*sakshi bhava* in Sanskrit). In the therapy world, this approach is adopted by

Acceptance and Commitment Therapy (ACT) and all the mindfulness-based interventions (MBIs).

PURE WITNESSING

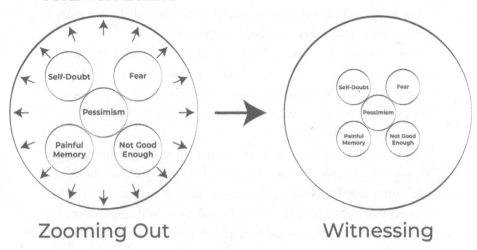

Witnessing is simple yet subtle. It's about taking a step back, gaining some space, and looking at the thought from a distance rather than being inside the thought. You are looking *at* the thought, not into the thought. You are aware of its content, but you are not *thinking* the content. And you are definitely not spinning it into a never-ending story or making important conclusions based on it. You let the thought be there without dwelling on it and let it go when it goes.

If this sounds a bit abstract, try to regard your thoughts as people walking by in a busy marketplace. You are aware of them, but you are not stopping and having a dialogue with everybody. And you are also not staring at and obsessing about any person—that wouldn't go well.

Other popular metaphors are that thoughts are like clouds in the sky or bubbles in a stream. Suppose the thought *I can't do this* comes up. You didn't invite that thought; it came on its own accord. It stays for some time, then it disappears by itself. The cloud will pass, the bubble will burst. Even if you want to keep it around forever, you can't—it has an expiration date, because another thought will replace it soon. While the thought is there, you have the option to believe it and weave it into a story or to just objectively recognize that the thought of *"I can't do this"* is here. Do you notice the difference?

Labeling thoughts like this is part of what is known as meta-awareness, which is the ability to be aware of the contents of your mind as they happen. In the beginning, such labeling is verbal; over time, it becomes more of a direct, wordless perception.

You can label thoughts individually or label a bunch of them as a single thing. To label them collectively, ask yourself: If all these thoughts and feelings were put into a movie, what would I name it? For example, you could call it the "Nobody likes me" story or the "I have no social skills" story.

Objectively labeling creates space between you and the thoughts. This space is the space of your freedom. It's the space that allows you to act differently from the suggestions of your thoughts and impulses. If there is no such space, then you are simply a product of your environment, as the loudest thought triggered in the moment is what will run the show.

In witnessing, you don't hold on to thoughts, and you don't push them away either. You don't suppress them or dialogue with them. And you definitely don't believe them and use them to define what you can or cannot do. All of these attitudes give power to the thought. Instead, you simply remain as the witness and observe. Retain your independence by remembering who you are—the witnessing awareness.

What happens when you do this? The thought remains there but loses the power to limit you. It ceases to define your experience. The inner critic can continue its lecture, but it just doesn't move you anymore. It doesn't stop you from doing what you want to do.

Does this mean you always just observe thoughts and never think them? No. That could be a problem. But it means you now have this option of stepping back and watching whenever you need an effective way of dealing with unhelpful thoughts. It also means you don't ruminate as much.

Research shows that low self-esteem is associated with greater negative self-related processing, including rumination.[1] In other words, the more you are thinking about yourself, the less likely you are to be experiencing real confidence. This is why witnessing, being the opposite of engaging in self-referential thoughts, helps you to be more confident.

When you are rooted in confidence, you are free from self-absorbed thinking and can fully focus on the challenge in front of you. Your energy is not engaged in thoughts of low self-esteem (I can't do this) or of self-importance (I'm great, I'm skillful; this will be a piece of cake). In a way, we could say that wise confidence is, actually, self-*less*.

Aids for Zooming Out

Sometimes you are so mesmerized by the contents of your thoughts that you may have trouble zooming out and just observing them as thoughts. Your meta-awareness is not strong enough, not trained enough; or perhaps some thoughts just slip in through the cracks more easily than others. You try labeling them, but in a split second you forget the label and find yourself again inside that thought bubble, taking its contents seriously and looking at reality through that lens.

When that is the case, you may need to play around with the thought in order to "break the spell." Here are some ideas from the world of Acceptance and Commitment Therapy (ACT).

- Repeat the thought in slow motion.

- Repeat the thought with a mocking voice.

- Sing your thoughts to the tune of "Row, Row, Row Your Boat."

- Answer back your thought with "Great, thanks for that!"

- Imagine your thought is a sentence on a computer screen, then play with it by changing the font, color, and formatting.

- Imagine that your thought is like an internet pop-up, then click to close it.

- Attribute color, weight, shape, and sound to your thought.

- Play the rebel and do the exact opposite of what the thought is suggesting.

Choose any of these strategies and try it for thirty to sixty seconds, and then notice what happens. Is the thought as powerful and alluring as it was before? Are you taking it as seriously as before?

Further, here are some ideas from the world of Eastern spirituality on how to break free from sticky thoughts:

- Ask yourself, What is this thought made of?

- Ask yourself, Who am I who is aware of this thought?

- Find out where this thought came from, and stay at its source.

- Replace the thought with the ongoing repetition of a sacred mantra.

- Say with conviction, This thought is not mine; this thought is not me.

All of these interventions involve a light engagement with the thought on top of the pure witnessing layer. They use imagination, verbalization, or inquiry to help you change your relationship with the thought without getting entangled in it.

THE NOT NOW TECHNIQUE[2]

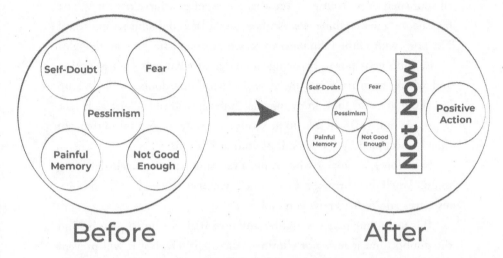

Before　　　　　　　　　After

This is a technique from my Mindful Self-Discipline framework. It helps you postpone the thoughts of self-doubt for later so you can stay focused and confident when you need to take action. It is also effective in dealing with distractions, excuses, cravings, fears, and impulses. It creates inner space and buys you time.

The concept is simple: instead of repressing or reframing negative thoughts, you just postpone them. You procrastinate thinking them. You notice them and say, Not now, and then immediately redirect your attention to something more important, here and now. Again, this approach involves adding a layer of action on top of pure witnessing—in this case, gently redirecting thoughts away on the grounds of "I'm busy now, but I will get to you later."

Once you get your headspace back by using "not now," focus wholeheartedly on the task at hand with conviction and enthusiasm. Feel that you are on the right path, that achieving your goal is just a matter of time. *Trust* that you are getting closer to your purpose with every step. *Know* that you can do it. Act based on your aspirational identity, as if no doubt ever existed.

The Not Now technique is the snooze button in your brain. It is procrastinating on things that are actually worth procrastinating! Procrastinate on doubt, fears, worries, anxiety, dramas, limiting beliefs, and distractions. Focus all your energies on your goal, on what you want to achieve right now, and hit "snooze" on everything else. Act first, doubt later. If doubts return, repeat "Not now" with a firm, calm inner voice, setting boundaries for your thoughts.

Reclaim your power by being in charge of what gets your attention and when. Eventually the mind will learn. Your doubts will give up knocking at your door, knowing that nobody will open, just as it happened for me. This will free up precious real estate in your mind that can then be occupied by the pursuit of your aspirations.

Not Now is an analysis-free zone, a vacation from your self-defeating mind. You'll be surprised how much you get done. You'll tap into resources you didn't know you had.

This technique may not resolve any potential emotional pain behind the doubts, and it may not eliminate them entirely, but it will prevent doubts and fears from spoiling your journey.

Not Now also helps you move forward with less friction, so you can taste wins sooner and thus build more confidence. Doubts may still exist, but they can't stop you from taking positive action—they cease to define you.

If you are having trouble implementing this technique broadly in your life, you can at least consider running a *doubt-free experiment*, during which you refuse to engage in any doubts. During the experiment, whenever a doubt, fear, or anxiety comes up, firmly say "not now!" and move forward. After the experiment ends, you can then review, learn, and question yourself or your chosen strategy, if needed.

This simple mindset shift works because you are seeing the practice as "just an experiment." Your mind can then cut you some slack, as it knows that this is a temporary thing and eventually it will be able to doubt again—it's just "not now."

The length of the doubt-free experiment depends on your needs. It could be an hour when you leave aside insecurities about your writing and just write. It could be a month when you follow a specific diet without stepping on the scale to see if it's working. It could be a year dedicated to a single business idea, snoozing other opportunities. Design your own doubt-free experiment and follow through wholeheartedly.

THE ROAR METHOD[3]

Sometimes you are not only dealing with thoughts but also powerful emotions or impulses. In this case, you are unlikely to be able to just witness them without getting involved, which means that your process will need to be a bit more elaborate.

Your conditioned identity has its emotional addictions. They could be fear, anxiety, shame, anger, grief, or impulses. When they come up, they can feel like a tsunami of energy uprooting you from your new ground and dragging you back to the old places. To deal with this, I teach my clients and students to use the ROAR Method, which I created years ago to help people deal with anxiety. Here is the simplified version:

- Recognize the emotion or urge that is present.
  Label it with statements like, "Anxiety is here" or "Boredom is here," or "Resentment is here." The simple act of recognizing a feeling and naming it can take the edge away.

- Observe it in your body as pure sensations. Where are they located? What are they like? See if they are hot or cool, focused or spread, shallow or deep, moving or stationary. Stay for some moments in the place where the sensations are the strongest.

- Accept the sensations as they are, without rejecting them, without aversion, and without contracting. Just stay with them. Create room for them. Let them be there, as if it makes no difference to you.

- Release the sensations with every out-breath.
  Imagine that you are breathing in and out through those sensations in your body, and that with every exhalation they are dissolving.

Do this for two to five minutes, and it will begin to shift your state. In most cases you will be ready to move forward and re-center on your designed identity. With regular practice, you will get so good at ROAR that you will be able to go through the process in just a few seconds.

This approach combines witnessing (steps one and three) with elements of embodiment (steps two and four). Refer to chapter 12 to learn more about embodiment. If you find the ROAR Method helpful, you can try the guided meditation version of it in the Mindful Self-Discipline app. Or you can download the ROAR wallpaper image to use on your phone for a constant reminder, using the link provided at the end of the book.

SUMMARY

Witnessing is taking a step back and getting some distance and objectivity from your thoughts—as opposed to dialoguing with them, questioning them, and reframing them. It is an exercise of meta-awareness, and it's aided by the practice of labeling thoughts and stories. It can also be aided by the use of imagination and metaphors.

When witnessing by itself is not enough, you can bring in a second layer to help you change your relationship with the thoughts. This could be anything that helps you see thoughts as just thoughts, such as singing them, mocking them, imagining them float away, or seeing their essential emptiness.

Other methods that are based on the key skill of witnessing include the Not Now technique, where we use willpower to postpone unhelpful thoughts, and the ROAR Method, where we combine witnessing with imagination and embodied interventions to release strong emotions.

11.

Imagination: Create Empowered States

Imagination is more important than knowledge.
Logic will take you from A to B. Imagination will take you everywhere.

—Albert Einstein

Live out of your imagination, not your history.

—Stephen Covey

The man who has no imagination has no wings.

—Muhammad Ali

Many people have a very limited conception of imagination. As a result, their *use* of imagination is also very limited. They see imagination only as "making things up," as child's play, as mental fantasies that should be kept in check by cold reason and facts. Rarely do they make use of imagination or realize its value.

Imagination is one of our core mental faculties—together with perception, memory, thought, and will. It is the act of creating "mental images," but that term needs to be broadly understood to encompass any type of perception. It is not only about *visual* images, with which it is commonly associated; you could imagine the presence of a sound, smell, taste, touch, movement, or feeling. There is also abstract imagination, which is creating thoughts and concepts. All creative thinking is an expression of imagination, as it is problem-solving. If you can't imagine, you can't come up with solutions or explanations. You can only react to the environment.

Imagination is the capacity of the mind to create an experience without external stimulus. As such, it is a true expression of the principle of living inside out. That experience can be the seed for creating change in your external or internal world.

If you can't imagine something new, you can't create it. If you can't imagine change, you can't achieve it. Everything that was ever invented existed first as an image in someone's mind. You create something within you, fall in love with that idea, then commit to manifesting it into a reality outside of you. Through repeated concentration, willpower, faith, and action, what was once "only" imagined becomes reality.

You can also use imagination for purposes that are solely internal, such as healing yourself, creating certain emotions, shifting your identity, doing spiritual practices, or programming new behaviors. You then feed and consolidate that imagination until it is as real as an experience that comes from outside the mind, via the senses.

In chapter 8, I introduced the concepts of concentration, willpower, and faith when we covered the Daily Alignment Practice. We also talked about the fourth element, feeling, which is basically the direct product of imagination. Now we can combine these four elements by saying that to produce any change, external or internal, we need two things: imagination and energy. We need to create the blueprint for our new reality, then breathe life into it. The trio of concentration, willpower, and faith is what gives weight to the imagination, gathering the energy needed to turn that idea into a lived reality.

REDEFINING REALITY

An effective exercise of imagination can create the same effects in your body, mind, and behavior as having that experience in reality. This is especially the case when the mental image is repeated with focus and intention, when there is a strong emotion associated with it, and when the mind is somewhat disengaged from the external world (i.e., not occupied with the senses).

The transformative power of imagination lies in the fact that your brain can't really tell the difference between what is happening in actuality and what is only happening in your memory or imagination. It treats all of these things the same way. Here are some examples:

- Your brain releases the same hormones when it encounters real social rejection as when it imagines it or remembers it vividly.[1] It's the same with many types of trauma[2]—for the brain, the past pain feels real *right now*, and it can't let go of that perception.

- Your brain treats false memories in exactly the same way it treats actual memories.[3]

- Your brain produces the same physiological changes whether you are in front of an attractive sexual partner or simply fantasizing about one.[4]

- Your mind can even heal your body if its imagination has been excited to believe that healing is taking place (the placebo effect). In like manner, it can create a nonexistent disease (the nocebo effect).[5]

- Feelings that were "imagined into existence" have the same psychological and physiological effects as feelings that arose spontaneously. (For more on this, listen to the TED Talk of psychologist Dan Gilbert, where he explores the idea of "manufacturing happiness" as an evolutionary development of our brain.[6])

- Experiments show that the imagined consumption of food can reduce actual consumption.[7]

- Research demonstrates that imagining that you have already achieved your goal can reduce motivation for the actual goal achievement.[8]

Joseph M. Carver, PhD, describes how psychologists at the University of Chicago studied three groups of basketball players.[9] Group one practiced foul shots each day for thirty days. Group two was instructed to "imagine" shooting foul shots each day for thirty days. Group three was instructed to do nothing. When tested, group three, who did nothing, had no improvement. Group one, those who actually practiced, improved 24 percent. Group two, those who only *imagined* practicing, improved 23 percent—even though they did not physically touch a basketball! This kind of experiment has been repeated in other areas of human activity with similar results.

When you do a meditation practice such as the lovingkindness meditation (from the Buddhist tradition) and feel love and joy in your heart, the same thing is happening in your body, mind, and hormones as if you were experiencing being loved in "real life." Why consider it real only when it is triggered by an external event but not when it is triggered internally? Why would it be real only when triggered by another person but not when triggered by ourselves? This is just a mental block, a limitation we have been conditioned to believe. If you hold on to it, you will severely limit your imagination.

All of this points to a clear conclusion: imagination is a mighty tool for you to shape your reality, both inside and out. Imagination is not about creating fake or unreal experiences, but it serves as a shortcut to create changes in yourself without depending on the external world. It is the most natural and powerful form of virtual reality. It frees you up to be what you want to be without needing to wait for the perfect external conditions. It is inherent in the practice of creating your new identity and *living inside out.*

"Okay, Giovanni, I'm now convinced of the transformative power of imagination, but I'm afraid of falling into self-delusion and looking like a fool." I'm glad you brought that up. Imagination and delusion are different things. Imagination is the process of creating a change through the power of your mind; delusion is when you believe that you have already completed that process and achieved a high level of success in it, when in fact you haven't.

If you imagine that you are Superman and then punch a stone wall, the wall will teach you a painful lesson: that you are deluded. But if you instead close your eyes and vividly imagine that you are as strong as Superman, use that imagination to create the *feeling* of superhuman strength in your muscles, and then go punch a sandbag—a much more reasonable experiment—you'll find that your punch has indeed gotten stronger. How much stronger? As much as your capacity to hold that imagination, that feeling, with concentration, willpower, and faith. That requires repeated practice, not a single spur of imagination and then assuming you are done.

Be committed to this practice, yet wise about your expectations.

Sharpening your passive imagination boosts your powers of perception; sharpening your active imagination boosts your powers of creation. Let's start by exploring the former.

PASSIVE IMAGINATION

Your conditioned identity—with all its history and limiting patterns—is encoded in your subconscious mind. So it's important to know how to understand and talk to your subconscious, using its own language. The subconscious mind communicates through images and symbols, not words or reason.

Passive imagination is the practice of receiving messages from the subconscious. When you set aside the analytical mind and turn your attention within—away from the world of mental chatter and sensory impressions—you make yourself available to a whole new mode of perception. You get to understand the psychology of your inner child and why it built the box.

There are many therapeutic modalities that use passive imagination to establish direct contact with the subconscious. Some of them are Internal Family Systems (IFS), Voice Dialogue, art therapy, Jungian dreamwork, the "Big Mind" process, and some forms of somatic therapy. In the world of spirituality, several wisdom traditions make use of passive imagination, although with a different purpose—such as Shamanic journeying, prayer, plant medicine, and some forms of meditation.

The way many of these techniques work is by allowing your subconscious to speak to you through the medium of inner parts, archetypes, or voices. To simplify things, let's call them our "parts." You are typically asked by a practitioner of these methodologies to get in contact with the *part* of you who is afraid of moving forward, or the *part* of you who is the inner critic, or the *part* of you who is feeling vulnerable and not confident. You are inviting the subconscious to give you access to that part, that "mode" of yourself, so you can learn from it, negotiate with it, or help it transform.

Your parts can show up as an image or a voice in your mind, as a sensation somewhere in your body, or even as a subtle inner knowingness. These are not consciously created nor a product of fantasy. Rather, they are real psychological constructs that are actively influencing your life and are now given the opportunity to show up to you via the medium of imagination.

For the purpose of experiencing more self-confidence, this process helps you get to know all parts of you that are involved with self-doubt, fear, anxiety, shaming, and the other obstacles to confidence. Then, through compassionate inner dialogue, you will:

- show gratitude to them, befriend them, and open a channel of communication

- understand what role they perform and what brought them into existence

- get each part to trust you, so you can reclaim their power and perform the same role, if still needed, in a wiser and more conscious manner. If that is not possible, at least ask the part what it needs from you so that it can give you some space.

The goal is to liberate your parts from unhelpful roles, help them grow, and create more harmony in your inner system. Sometimes that means finding a more functional way to satisfy those original needs; other times it could be coming to a point where that part realizes that its role is no longer required. As part of this process, you as awareness (the Self) begin to take charge. I like to call this self-mastery.

In the past, I've gone through this process with the help of a therapist and coach skilled in IFS, and I found it extremely insightful and liberating. Based on my experience, I don't believe that this method can be effectively taught through a book for self-application. Sure, I can explain the broad process and share some of the common questions used, but this is very different from being guided by someone who knows how to respond to what is spontaneously arising within you in the moment. Especially because this can be a very emotionally triggering process, it is best to initially practice it with a trusted guide. After some guided experience with this technique, you may be able to do this inner work yourself.

One of the key lessons from this work is that all parts of you are good. Even the inner critic, the complainer, the saboteur—all of them have good intentions. They are seeking your well-being in their own way, or at least trying to protect you, either skillfully or unskillfully. These parts cannot be destroyed, and attempting to do so will only make them shapeshift into something else to escape the eyes of your conscious mind and thus live on. While they cannot be destroyed, they can be *transformed* through the power of awareness and inner dialogue.

Thoughts and feelings are the by-products of our identity and all its parts. In the mindset work (chapter 9), we are trying to manage and reframe our thoughts by working at their level. In the witnessing (chapter 10), we are zooming out and letting the thoughts be, without them affecting or controlling us. Now, in passive imagination, we are having a dialogue with the source of our thoughts, feelings, desires, and fears—our *parts*. These are three different ways of dealing with unhelpful mental patterns, and they are presented in this book from the most external to the most internal: thoughts → meta-awareness → subconscious.

All these methodologies depend on the power of your awareness. If your awareness is clear, sharp, and stable, you will be able to do this type of inner work more easily and quickly. This is why the practice of meditation, as a great training tool for awareness, is essential for effectively applying these techniques. We'll cover meditation in the last chapter of the Awareness Pillar. Until then, let's have a look at the other main way of using imagination.

ACTIVE IMAGINATION

This world is but a canvas to our imagination.

—Henry David Thoreau

If passive imagination is like reading, active imagination is more like writing. It is what is more typically associated with imagination—an act of creation. Most people use this faculty for creating art, visualizing possibilities, learning, and problem-solving. In this chapter, however, we are focusing on using imagination to create an internal state, produce an emotion, bring about healing, or program a certain behavior.

You see this approach everywhere. Most Olympic athletes use some form of visualization practice. Martial artists too. In therapy, there is Jungian active imagination work and self-hypnosis. In the world of personal development, there is great emphasis on the practices of affirmation and visualization. In the world of spirituality, there is the practice of forming a resolution or sankalpa (see chapter 6), especially through meditation techniques such as Yoga Nidra and Mantra Sadhana.

As you can see, active imagination is very different from the practice of witnessing, covered in the previous chapter. Witnessing is completely passive—it is seeing things as they are and letting them be that way. Imagination is engaging with the subconscious and creating. You witness with detachment and calmness that which you want to disappear. You imagine with energy and intention that which you want to create.

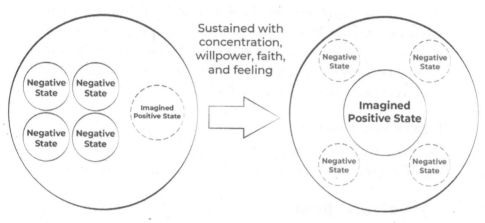

Active Imagination

In the beginning

Negative State · Negative State · Negative State · Negative State · Imagined Positive State

Sustained with concentration, willpower, faith, and feeling

After some practice

Imagined Positive State · Negative State · Negative State · Negative State · Negative State

Witnessing is an awareness practice, while imagination is a willpower practice. Wise Confidence, and the larger framework of Mindful Self-Discipline, is the synthesis of both.

Now let's get to some practical imagination exercises that can help you use your imagination to shift your state. There is no right or wrong here; these are just basic templates. Whatever imagery helps you create the desired shift can be used. This process is completely flexible and personal.

Shifting Your Present and Your Future

Imagining Confidence

Create, through imagination and visualization, the felt sense of being confident. Feel it in your body, mind, and heart. Then see yourself effectively performing the task that you need to perform. Positive expectations for success produce positive effects. Expecting that you will be able overcome your challenges makes it more likely that you will. Just make sure to not dwell on the end state of having already achieved it because, as we've already discussed, this is shown to decrease motivation.

Removing Obstacles to Confidence

Identify your main obstacle to self-confidence. It could be that you think you are not attractive enough, or that you came from a poor family, or that in the past people may have bullied you and you think you didn't succeed at anything. Then imagine your life without that obstacle, as if it simply doesn't exist. Or imagine that you're putting it in a rocket and sending it to outer space, never to return. Feel how it would actually feel. Then act accordingly! Choose to live that life today.

POWER Visualization

This method is about visualizing yourself meeting obstacles and effectively overcoming them. The step-by-step instructions are included in chapter 8.

Releasing Negative Thoughts

When you are experiencing a negative thought or emotion, you can use imagination to suggest to your mind that such thought or emotion is being dissolved. Let's suppose that a thought of self-doubt comes up and won't leave you alone. You can visualize writing that thought down on a piece of paper and then burning it or shredding it. Some people find it helpful to actually do this as a small ritual. Or you could imagine placing that thought on a leaf on the surface of a gentle stream and watching it float away. In the Yoga tradition, there is the practice of visualizing a light coming from your third eye and burning that thought into nothing.

Meeting Your Future Self

Imagine that you are meeting your future self. It is the wiser version of yourself, some years from now, who has effectively gone through the challenges you are now facing. See yourself meeting him/her face to face and asking a question. Remain in a state of receptivity, fully open and nonjudgmental, waiting for an answer without any impatience. Repeat the question if needed, and be constantly vigilant that the analytical mind doesn't come up to say its opinion.

Shifting Your Past

It's true that we can't change our factual past. But our identity, our *parts*, are not built on facts, but on stories, interpretations, and beliefs. This is something imagination can act on.

In the past you might have been repeatedly mocked, abused, or even beaten up for expressing your opinions. These experiences can naturally lead to a mental pattern of fear and shyness about saying what you think or asking for what you want. However, if you manage to convince yourself—not only intellectually but *experientially*—that you actually grew up in a supportive environment that encouraged you to say what you think and be authentic, you will naturally feel more confident. You will have higher self-esteem. You may still objectively remember that there were cases of abuse when you shared your opinion, but in your mind they will feel like unimportant exceptions and will have no more emotional charge to them.

"But, Giovanni, seriously, isn't this lying to yourself?" you might say. No. The "truth" about your life is not fixed, but constructed; it is not objective, but subjective. You can use the power of imagination to rebuild yourself, to construct a better story and foundation for your life. This is not as far-fetched as it sounds. Everybody does this on one level or another, but mostly unconsciously. I'm inviting you to do it on purpose.

I'm in good company here. Dr. Daniel P. Brown, PhD, is an expert in developmental trauma and served as a faculty member at Harvard Medical School for nearly four decades. Dr. Brown created the "Ideal Parents Protocol," a visualization practice in which you see yourself having grown up in a family different from your family of origin. You imagine scenes of your "ideal parents" interacting with you in ways that make you feel safe and protected, showing emotional connection to you, comforting you, expressing delight in your every action, and positively encouraging you to be all you can be.

The goal with this practice is to remap your emotional foundation to one that is positive and stable. You keep doing that with your imagination repeatedly, creating a lived experience within your mind and heart, until you begin to operate out of that new model in actual life. At this point, the old model becomes irrelevant, even though you may still be objectively aware of it.

In like manner, you can use imagination to remap any past experiences that are preventing you from being your best self. It doesn't happen overnight, but it's a very direct approach to healing. The possibilities for this approach are endless.

Making It All Work

It is better to start any of the above exercises with a short meditation practice, so your mind is more clear and internalized. This will help your mental imagery be stronger and more stable. If your mind is distracted and scattered, the imagination won't gather enough energy to get a life of its own.

Imagination is autosuggestion. It is our ability to create an internal reality "out of thin air." But if the mind is scattered, if the autosuggestion is weak, or if there is hesitation about its efficacy, then that internal reality will not be sustained long enough in consciousness to produce any real effect.

In other words: not all imagination is equal. To be effective, your imagination needs to be *empowered* by concentration, willpower, and faith. So please understand that for the exercises explained in this chapter to fully work, you will need to regularly practice them over a period of time until that particular mental image gets consolidated within you.

Learn how to be patient and disciplined about these practices, and you can reap their fruits. Learn to hold your mental images with full attention, with full *intention*, and with the belief that they are absolutely real. This is where imagination meets reality—nay, creates it.

12.

Embodiment: Find Confidence in Your Body

No one is born with confidence.
Those people around you who radiate confidence,
who have conquered worry,
who are at ease everywhere and all the time,
acquired their confidence, every bit of it.

—Dale Carnegie

You can create ecstasy at will
by changing your physiology.

—Tony Robbins

Only the person who can roar like a lion
can be said to be alive.

—Narayan Dutt Shrimali

The three previous chapters covered different ways we can work with the mind by shifting thoughts, witnessing them, or creating states through imagination. This chapter is all about using your *body* to affect the mind.

Embodiment and somatic psychology are a growing trend in therapy and coaching that emphasizes practices that explore the body-mind connection, especially for healing trauma. The principles of embodiment are also used in Mindfulness and the Hatha Yoga tradition, but for different purposes. In all cases, the premise is simple: every emotion, feeling, or state exists both as a thought in the mind and as a sensation or movement in the body. So if you change the body at a subtle level, you will change the related emotions and states. You experienced this in steps two and four of the ROAR Method (chapter 10).

There are many modalities of embodied or somatic practices used for healing and releasing negative emotions. In this book, we will approach the topic from the other end: how to use the body-mind connection to create *positive* mental states. We will explore practices that allow you to create the feeling of self-confidence and anchor that experience in your body so it lasts longer.

If you meet challenges when you are in a state of contraction or low energy, you will not feel very confident about your capacity to tackle them. On the other hand, if you meet the same challenges when you are in a state of expansion, high energy, and fire, they will not feel as scary or overwhelming. You will feel that you have the resources to overcome the challenge, so you can more easily trust yourself.

The lesson here is this: first shift your physical and emotional state, *then* deal with challenges. Don't decide what you can or cannot do from a contracted, low-energy state. In order to solve the problem, you need to become bigger than the problem. You need to free yourself from that little box and see the challenge from a different place. You make a decision to do something from an empowered state of aspiration and self-belief, and then use self-discipline to remain aligned with that commitment even after that state subsides.

The feeling of confidence is the feeling of strength, resourcefulness, and aliveness. It's the refreshing feeling that you can do anything, move anywhere, conquer any challenge, and explore any new world. It's an expanded and high-energy state.

There are different ways to get to that state of high energy and expansion. One way is using your mind—you could remember your core strengths and tap into them, or you could remember your core aspirations and draw energy from them, or you could use your mindset or imagination to shift your state. Another way is to create that change in your body, through movement, breathing, postures, or subtle energy shifts, which is the topic of this chapter. Sometimes a combination of both approaches is the best way forward. Let me tell you a story that illustrates this point.

When I was in middle school and early high school, I experienced many incidents of bullying. I was the skinny nerd, often introspective and alone, in classes full of older kids who had in muscles and aggression what they lacked in brains. So it's easy to see why I'd be a good target. It's like there was something about me that was invisibly sending the message "Bully me!" to the boys around me.

Until one day it all began to change. First, I made a decision: "I am *done* with this. I am not going to passively accept bullying anymore. I will fight back, and even if I get beaten up, at least I will have given them a hard time and get to keep my dignity." I got involved in four fights with four different bullies. There was blood and broken bones. It wasn't pretty, but it was necessary. I established clear boundaries.

Second, shortly after that decision, I began taking Kung Fu classes, which helped consolidate that change. Nobody knew about it, but suddenly people stopped bothering me. There was something different about how I carried myself. Not so much because I knew killer moves that could finish any fight—I didn't yet. But because I felt different and saw myself differently. My posture and my movements were sending a different message. I didn't look like an easy target anymore.

Changing your mind will change your body, but changing your body will also change your mind. Of these two, it is often easier to follow the bottom-up approach of working with the body. If your awareness is not sharp enough, awakened enough, or stable enough, that might be your only option.

AWAKENING CONFIDENCE IN YOUR BODY

Let's do a quick experiment. Think of a time in the recent past when you were experiencing the opposite of self-confidence—perhaps self-doubt, anxiety, nervousness, or insecurity. This shouldn't be a severe incident with an intensity of ten out of ten, which could be traumatizing to relive; instead, choose a milder experience, but one that is still very real. Remember that state and what triggered it. Remember how you were feeling. Remember your self-talk. Do so until that state is present here and now.

Then pay attention to what is going on in your body. Can you locate where the unpleasant emotion is "living"? For some people it is a sense of contraction or coldness in the chest. Others feel it as a sensation of shrinking or sinking in all over the body. It could also be a sense of fogginess in your head or a trembling in the legs. It shows up as different things for different people. Try to identify the strongest cue of this state in your body.

Once you have identified the cues, begin to study those sensations with curiosity, like a scientist. Focus on them intently, and ask yourself the following questions:

- Is it warm or cool?

- Is it shallow or deep?

- Is it focused or spread out?

- Is it tingly or sharp?

- Is it numb or alive?

- Is it still or moving?

- If there is movement, is it spinning, swirling, vibrating, curling?

- If you could attribute a color to it, what color would it be?

These questions train your awareness to become sharper, more nuanced, and more discerning when it comes to your body. This is similar to the Observe step of the ROAR Method (chapter 10). Now you know exactly what the opposite of self-confidence feels like in your body, and you can identify it with clarity whenever you notice any of its signs showing up.

Now, what do you do with these sensations? Using self-suggestion, coupled with your body awareness, you shift them to their opposite. For example, if self-doubt feels like a black ball of contraction in your chest that's cold and still, you use your imagination to alter each of those attributes. You create the feeling that what was cold is now getting warm, what was still is now moving freely, and the black ball of contraction is now expanding into white light spreading all over your body. By shifting these sensations you will shift the related emotions.

Now let's do the opposite exercise. Remember a time in your life when you felt really confident. Or it could be a time when you felt one of the other strengths connected to confidence, such as courage, energy, determination, or conviction. Remember everything you can about that time in your life—where you were, what you were doing, who you were with, what was at stake, and any other important details. Remember your self-talk and how you were feeling. Make it as real as possible, until you feel that empowered feeling again, here and now.

If you don't have any memories to back up the confidence you want to feel, then use your imagination. You could imagine what such confidence feels like, and embrace that state. If that doesn't work, you can think of someone, real or fictitious, who has that type of confidence, then imagine that you are absorbing or mirroring that way of being inside yourself. Embody that. In Mindful Self-Discipline, we call that "Absorb the Virtue."

Then locate that feeling in your body. If it's in more than one place, select the place where it is strongest. Focus on that feeling, and get a full resolution picture of what it is by using the same questions as before. At this point, you have a very clear physical handle for the quality you wish to have.

Embodied Confidence

Before: Vague bodily awareness

After: Confidence in body and mind

For a more holistic experience of this quality, you can also observe how confidence shows up in your mind and in your heart by becoming aware of the thoughts and feelings it creates. Then you will have three handles for this state: body, mind, and heart. Spend some time dwelling in this state, with awareness of all the aspects of the experience of confidence.

Why is this useful? Because then whenever you want to be confident, you can re-create this positive state by internally kindling the physical sensations of confidence (body handle), and optionally supporting that effort by evoking the self-talk of confidence (mind handle) and the feelings of confidence (heart handle). In other words, you can now generate confidence at will! Every time you do that, it becomes a little easier. Practice shifting to it multiple times a day. With some practice over time, you'll get to a point where you have the button of confidence just a tap away.

ANCHORING CONFIDENCE

By going through this process of identifying and strengthening the three, you will re-create the positive state of confidence. However, wouldn't it be great to have a shortcut, something you can use to quickly tap into that state? That is what an anchor is.

Anchoring is a term used in neurolinguistic programming (NLP) for pairing an internal state with a physical touch or gesture so that in the future you can re-create that state by repeating that touch or gesture. To establish an anchor, do that gesture when you are experiencing the peak of the positive state and release it once it begins to fade. That teaches your nervous system that the two are related. The more intense the state and the more precise the timing, the stronger the anchor will be.

For example, let's say you want to have clenched fists as an anchor for confidence. Every time you experience self-confidence—either spontaneously or via the practice covered in this chapter—you'll then immediately clench your fists as that state peaks. Like this, you make a strong association between the state and the gesture. This could be aided by telling yourself, *When I clench my fists, I am filled with confidence.* As per the guidelines for affirmations in chapter 8, you need to say this with concentration, willpower, faith, and feeling.

After establishing this link a few times, you can automatically produce the state of confidence simply by clenching your fists. While this may not work every single time, it is definitely a shortcut worth building.

Your anchor needs to be specific to the state you want to tap into; otherwise, it will be ineffective. For this reason, using a thumbs-up gesture would not be a good anchor because we use that gesture in many occasions, for purposes other than re-creating an internal state. Likewise, your anchor should not be something that happens all the time because then the brain would get desensitized to that trigger.

The idea of anchoring is much older than NLP. And it need not be limited to a gesture or touch. It could be an image, word, smell, movement, or object. Here are some examples:

- Image (external): looking at your toes to anchor a state of being grounded
- Image (internal): visualizing a mountain to anchor resilience or stillness
- Word: repeating your Power Word to yourself to evoke that strength

- Smell: inhaling the scent of sandalwood or incense to anchor peace of mind

- Sound: ringing a bell to anchor presence (as is done in many temples)

- Movement: snapping your fingers to help you let go of a negative thought

You can use whatever anchor works for you and is easily accessible. Personally, I have an image anchor for the state of bliss—I can basically close my eyes, visualize that sacred image, and fill my body with bliss within a minute. In Kung Fu, there is a martial greeting which represents the state of the warrior with all its virtues (courage, strength, dignity, etc.). In Mindful Self-Discipline, many of us use a wristband to remind ourselves of our aspirations. Yogis sit in a special posture that helps them achieve deep meditative states. Married couples wear a ring as a constant reminder of their commitment. In all these cases, though, the anchor can lose its effectiveness if the association with its purpose is not deliberately kept alive.

All of these are examples of using an anchor to reproduce a state or to remind you of an intention. The possibilities for anchoring are endless. The important thing to remember is that anchoring is a *process*. You may not experience results immediately, but with repetition and patience, willpower and belief, you'll definitely get there.

THE LION MUDRA

A *mudra* is a gesture used in the world of meditation and Yoga to help you tap into certain inner states. Yogis have found, through extensive experimentation, that the way the hands and fingers are kept in meditation have a subtle effect on the mind—although not everybody will notice it immediately.

Be that as it may, the point is that a mudra can be used to anchor the state of confidence. For this purpose, I have created a mudra that symbolizes the principles of both Wise Confidence and Mindful Self-Discipline.

I call it the LION mudra, which is short for *living inside-out now*. Here is how to make it:

Whenever you are experiencing self-confidence, practicing your willpower, or shifting into your aspirational identity, bring your hands together like the image above, for a minute, to anchor that state. This gesture is modest enough to be adopted anywhere without making you feel awkward—only you know its meaning and purpose.

If you are sensitive, you may immediately notice how bringing your hands together in this manner, with this intention, helps you feel more calm and centered. If not, don't worry. You will get there once the anchor is fully established.

You can anchor a state with any random gesture, yet the LION mudra is much more than a random gesture. There is a lot of thought and symbolism behind it.

- Your hand shape resembles the pointer of a compass, which is a symbol for purpose and direction.

- The triangle is pointing up, representing the movement of breaking free from the gravity of the conditioned identity and elevating yourself toward your aspirations.

- The three corners of the triangle remind us of the three pillars of Aspiration, Awareness, and Action.

- Finally, uniting both your hands in this manner, with all fingers touching, invites you to close the gap between who you are now and who you want to be, actualizing your ideal self here and now.

RAISING YOUR ENERGY LEVELS

Energy is power, life, and vitality. It is much easier to feel confident if you experience abundant energy in your body and mind. In fact, confidence is a type of abundance. When you have more money than you need, you experience financial abundance. When you have more time than things to do, you experience time abundance. When you have more intelligence than your work requires, you experience intellectual abundance. When you have more energy and skill than the challenge demands, you experience confidence, a type of emotional abundance.

When you are full of energy, there is a natural sense of confidence and power within you. You feel as though you can conquer the world. You naturally believe in yourself. You are happy to be alive. You feel healthy and motivated. You also become more capable of digesting your life—and your food—quickly. No more staying stuck or sluggish.

When we were born in this world, we could only lie down. To be able to sit, we needed to apply some energy. Then, after some time, to be able stand, more energy was required. Then walking, running, and jumping. This is the law of life: you need more energy to unlock each new stage. To get to the next stage in your life, in your development, in your journey, you will need more energy. Confidence is a by-product of that. If you can't generate energy, if you can't focus and direct your energy, you'll end up staying stuck where you are.

In a nutshell: to have more energy is to have more life. It's to be able to do more, live more, *be* more. Energy enables you to express your hidden potential, reach further, and live a bigger life. It activates deeper resources in your brain and produces a brighter light (to use the electricity metaphor from chapter 1).

Raising your vitality is a complex topic with many variables. Your energy level is influenced by several things. Some of them you can't control, such as your age or genetics. Yet there are plenty of factors that influence your energy level and *are* under your control—such as your diet, sleep routine, environment, life philosophy, sense of purpose, mindset, goals you pursue, emotional patterns, and other lifestyle habits.

Within the context of the mind-body connection, there are also multiple approaches that can stimulate your inner fire and clear emotional blockages so you can raise your energy levels. These include yoga, dance, Pilates, qigong, massage, tai chi, and some styles of martial arts—each of which is a world of its own.

I encourage you to explore the approaches you feel attracted to and see what works for you. Whatever helps you feel more vibrant and full of energy will also help you with self-confidence. I encourage you to check out "The Yoga of Confidence" in Appendix 1, where I share specific postures and breathing exercises from the Hatha Yoga tradition. In my personal experience, and also in that of some of my clients, these exercises can work wonders in this regard—which is why I still practice some of them daily.

13.

Meditation: Feel Secure Within Yourself

Inner stillness is the key to outer strength.

—Jared Brock

When meditation is mastered,
the mind is unwavering like the
flame of a candle in a windless place.

—The Bhagavad Gita

Nothing can harm you as much
as your own thoughts, unguarded.

—The Buddha

The skills developed through meditation are foundational to every other personal development practice. Meditation boosts the effectiveness of all the techniques taught in this book, especially the ones in the Awareness pillar. But what is it exactly?

Meditation is a mental exercise that involves relaxation, awareness, and focus. It is to the mind what physical exercise is to the body. The practice is usually done individually in a still, seated position, with the eyes closed. Meditation thus often involves bodily stillness. But there are also ways to do walking meditation and to integrate mindfulness into other activities, in what we could call "dynamic stillness."

Imagine that you have the superpowers of calmness and awareness. You have great self-control and can remain cool and collected even in the midst of a storm. You don't flinch when you face big challenges. You have enough space within you, enough pause, to not be carried away by fears, anxieties, and negative self-talk. With all of this, won't you naturally be more confident? You definitely will. Others will see that in you, admire you for it, and secretly wish they could do the same.

A solid meditation practice can do all that for you. And it's for everybody, not only for those who can "empty their minds." You don't need to be a calm person to meditate, just like you don't need to be strong to go to the gym. To practice meditation, you also don't need to be religious, hold any special beliefs, or sit in an exotic, difficult pose. Meditation is not a selfish indulgence nor an invitation to run away from your life. Quite the contrary, it is an essential practice to keep yourself healthy, sane, present, and happy.

Now, let's unpack some of the main ways how meditation can help you become more confident. While there are many different styles of meditation, each with its own goals and effects, they all share some common benefits.

MEDITATION BENEFITS FOR SELF-CONFIDENCE[1]

Gives You Calmness

Calmness begets confidence, and confidence begets calmness. When you are aware of your strengths and resources and feel optimistic about the outcomes of an undertaking, you will not be agitated about taking action. You'll do so calmly and firmly. It also works the other way around: if you are able to maintain calmness even in adversity, you'll be sending a message to your nervous system that you've got it all under control. Meditation helps you master the art of remaining cool under pressure.

I speak from experience. Because of my meditation practice, I now always have the option to be at ease, almost regardless of the circumstances. My body is often very relaxed, open, and calm—even in the midst of a heated discussion or direct confrontation. Multiple times I've witnessed the confronting person feel confused and annoyed at how little I've been triggered by their words and behavior. They would approach me feeling arrogantly righteous, then leave disappointed and angry because they couldn't move me out of my center.

How is this level of calm possible? If my mind and energy begin to contract or get agitated, I'm aware of it. I then immediately release that pattern before it has the chance to establish itself, in a way similar to the ROAR Method. After having done this many times, it becomes second nature and doesn't require much effort. It's like the constant rebalancing that we unconsciously do when riding a bicycle.

I was not born this way. I had a short fuse as a child, as some members of my household also had (and still have). As a result of regular meditation and personal growth exercises, over the years, I've been able to overcome that family pattern. With disciplined practice, this equanimity is also possible for you. You can get to a point where you feel so calm and unaffected that your presence exudes unbreakable confidence.

Gives You the Superpower to Pause

During meditation you practice slowing things down, observing your mind, and pausing whenever you get entangled in your thoughts or feelings. This ability helps you with self-confidence big time. How? Whenever you are going down the rabbit hole of self-doubt and negativity, you can then pause and zoom out instead of getting stuck in your old conditioning and disempowering yourself even further.

Rather than fighting with your negative self-talk—which taxes the brain—meditation teaches you to be aware of it and accept it, but without believing it. This not only saves you energy but is also more effective. It shows you the difference between experiencing a thought and acting on it. When that space between you and your thoughts and emotions is present, by virtue of your meditation practice, then you have the freedom to act on them or not—you are in control. As a result, you can choose to move forward based on your aspirational identity rather than your conditioned identity, based on your values rather than your limitations.

Trains Your Awareness and Willpower

Most styles of meditation involve an exercise not only of awareness but also of willpower. This is especially true in the case of concentration-based meditation. Let's say you sit for meditation with a strong intention to focus on your breathing, moment after moment, without getting distracted. Forming that resolve is, in itself, an expression of willpower. Then you need your awareness to stay fully awake and vigilant, continuously monitoring your mind to see whether your attention is still with the breath or not. Whenever you notice your attention has wandered, you then interrupt that thought-current and re-establish your attention on your breath, reaffirming your intention to keep it there.

As you can see, meditation is a constant exercise of pause, awareness, and willpower—the elements of the PAW Method! These three core skills are essential for practicing any other personal development technique; without them, nothing will work. Besides, willpower, in itself, already brings self-confidence with it because it makes you feel stronger, more capable, and more resilient.

Helps You Change Your Narrative

As we've covered in previous chapters, your self-talk, beliefs, and mindsets are habits, not truths. So they can be changed. You unlearn bad habits of thought by not paying attention to the old ways of thinking and either replacing them with more useful ways of thinking (chapter 9) or just letting them pass (chapter 10).

When the voice of fear comes up and says, "Don't do that! You will fail, and it will be horrible," you have a choice. You can listen to it, believe it, and follow it by doubting yourself and not taking action. Or you can ignore it, let it be there in the periphery, and take confident action regardless. You can even deliberately bring up the voice of courage in you and feed it with your attention.

You may not be able to control the voices that come up nor the stories they tell—but you can choose what you do with them. You can decide which voice gets the mic and for how long. The voices inside of you that you stop paying attention to will weaken and eventually disappear; the voices that you pay attention to will strengthen and come to life. I call this the *Law of Attention*. Attention gives life to whatever it touches.

What are you paying attention into existence in your life?

Here again we see the value of meditation on your journey of self-confidence. By teaching you how to control your attention, meditation enables you to break free from the conditioned identity by starving it of attention and to strengthen your aspirational identity by feeding it with attention.

THE THREE PILLARS OF MEDITATION[2]

The three pillars of meditation are the key areas you need to focus on to have an enjoyable and effective meditation practice. If you develop these pillars, your practice will flourish, and you will experience the benefits. But if you don't—if even one of them is missing—then the benefits you get will be limited.

The three pillars of meditation are habit, technique, and transformation. In short, you need to practice meditation *daily*, with the optimal *technique*, and then deliberately apply the skills you get from meditation to *transform* your daily life.

Habit

Meditation is not like physical exercise, where you can get away with practicing only two or three times a week. It's actually the sort of thing you need to do *daily*—just like eating, sleeping, showering, and brushing your teeth. It's in *that* category of activities.

Why? Because thoughts are spinning in your head nonstop, and the inner critic doesn't go on vacation. Your impulses and limiting beliefs are active on a daily basis, and your conditioned identity is there 24/7. So you need to meditate on a daily basis too. Otherwise, it will be difficult to reverse years of negative patterns of thought and emotion.

What happens if you meditate only once a week? You will surely experience some benefits. Right after the meditation, you will likely feel more calm, centered, and focused. You may immediately feel clearer and more resilient. But that state won't last—because once a week is not enough for you to get real momentum in the practice. It will not be transformational for you.

Suppose you want to boil some water. You need to leave your kettle on the heat for five minutes so the water will boil. But instead you leave it on for two minutes, then turn it off and come back to it the following week to turn it on for two more minutes. You may do that for all the weeks of your life, but the water will never boil. After a weeklong break in the process, the water completely cools down to the baseline so you are starting the process from scratch again.

In a way, meditation practice is like that. That is why it's essential to practice it every day, even if for just five minutes. If you do that, you will build some momentum in your practice, and it will grow. A daily habit is what makes the difference between having a practice that *feels good when you do it* and one that can actually transform your life.

Building a daily habit of meditation is all about self-discipline and following some simple habit-building principles. If you need some guidance around this, I encourage you to read my book *Mindful Self-Discipline*.

Technique

The second pillar is having the *right technique* for meditation. This has nothing to do with the dogmatic beliefs of some meditation groups, who preach that their style is superior to all others. Rather, right technique means finding the style that is optimal *for you* at this stage in your life. Meditation is an incredibly versatile practice, with many centuries of history. There are hundreds of styles of meditation, each of them with a different focus, process, and benefits.

When most people think of meditation techniques, what comes to mind is either watching the breath or repeating a mantra. Those techniques are great, and they do work for some people, but they may not be optimal for you. Until you experiment with a variety of styles, you can't know if there is a more effective technique out there for you.

There is no "one size fits all" in meditation, yet that is the way it is often taught by many teachers and courses. While most meditation techniques do share a great number of common benefits, there is still a big difference between practicing a technique that just *works for you* and practicing a technique that is *optimal* for you, just like there is a big difference between an okay job and your ideal job. Finding the right style of meditation for you matters a lot.

It is beyond the scope of this book to explore the main styles of meditation and how to choose the ideal practice for you. Besides, I don't think a book is the best way to go about this process. Ideally you would want to use guided meditations or be mentored systematically by a teacher who is knowledgeable in the different styles. Of course, you can also do this by yourself by doing your own research. Experiment with different techniques and philosophies for some time and see what moves the needle for you the most. Or check out the "Going Deeper" section at the end of this book for a more supported journey.

Transformation
The third pillar is *transformation*, which is applying your meditation skills in daily life. Meditation is not only what you do while sitting on a cushion for a few minutes every day—it needs to be integrated into your life. When that happens, the benefits multiply, and you experience the real goal of the practice: self-transformation.

In the journey of self-confidence, this means utilizing the skills honed through meditation to enhance your ability to effectively apply the techniques presented in this book. Every time you meditate, you are cultivating important internal skills, such as

- pausing
- self-awareness
- focus

- willpower

- relaxation

- zooming out

- letting go of unhelpful thoughts

- managing emotional states

- self-acceptance

Chances are that one or more of your Power Words are directly trained in meditation.

It is true that if you practice meditation daily, with the right technique for you, over time some things will automatically begin to change. The way you see the world, the way you see yourself, and how you interact with people around you—all will change. But you can greatly accelerate this process if you do it *on purpose*.

The key message of the transformation pillar is that your daily life needs to be an extension of your meditation. You need to take your meditation beyond the cushion if you want real change.

USEFUL TECHNIQUES FOR CONFIDENCE

Any meditation technique that helps you develop greater pause, awareness, and willpower will be beneficial to your self-confidence. In this book we have also covered some specific meditation practices that are more directly connected with self-confidence, such as *Yoga Nidra* (chapter 6), the ROAR Method (chapter 10), and active imagination (chapter 11).

Next, we will briefly cover some other practices related to the different aspects of building confidence. If you want guided meditations for these techniques and others related to self-confidence and self-discipline, check out the "Going Deeper" section at the end of this book.

Trataka

This technique, developed in the Yogic tradition, involves steadily gazing at an object. It is one of the most excellent exercises for strengthening focus and willpower. A variety of objects are recommended for this practice, depending on the goal. For the purpose of growing your confidence, I suggest you use a candle flame or a mirror.

For candle gazing, place the candle in front of you at eye level, about two or three feet away. The room should be somewhat dark and without draughts so the flame doesn't flicker. Sit still in a comfortable meditation posture, close your eyes, and take a few deep breaths to calm your mind. Then open your eyes and gaze intently at the top of the wick. Your gaze should be relaxed but still, blinking as little as possible. Focus your eyes and mind, moment after moment, on the flame. When your eyes get tired or begin to water, close them for a couple of minutes, then go for another round. Do this for five to twenty minutes.

The practice of mirror gazing is similar. The only differences are that the room should be dimly lit (instead of dark) and you are gazing at your own reflection in the mirror, either at your right eye or the spot between your eyebrows. Breathe very slow, long breaths, as this will help you deepen your concentration. After a while, your face image may look distorted, turn black, or even completely disappear. These are all normal effects of this exercise, and you need not worry about them.

These practices will develop willpower, concentration, and a special glow in your eyes—together with the confidence that comes from these things. Trataka also improves your memory and visualization skills, calms anxiety, and helps with insomnia.

Loving-kindness (Metta)

If you struggle not only with confidence but also with low self-esteem and tend to be really hard on yourself, then try the loving-kindness meditation. This practice comes from the Buddhist tradition, where it is known by the Pali word *metta*.

In the first part of the meditation, you generate feelings of loving-kindness by either remembering times when you felt unconditional love or by imagining what it would feel like. Once the genuine feeling has been kindled, you then focus on it fully, allowing it to grow and take root in you. This feeling then becomes the object of your meditation.

Then we get to the second part, where you project that feeling toward someone. In the case of healing and self-confidence, that someone is yourself! It can be helpful to visualize yourself, then say, *May you be happy. May you be safe. May you be at peace!* Say it with feeling and intention.

Mantra Meditation

Mantra is a universal tool of meditation. Buddhists, Hindus, Christians, Sufis, and Jains, all use mantras. A mantra is a word, syllable, or short sentence that is repeated during meditation. The repetition may be done out loud, whispering, or simply in your mind.

Traditionally, a mantra is always repeated in its original, classic language (Sanskrit, Tibetan, Chinese, Arabic, or Latin). It is so because the most important thing is believed to be the actual vibration produced by the sacred sound and its effects on our consciousness. In modern times, however, people have adapted the idea of mantra meditation to instead repeat words and sentences in their mother tongue, and then the emphasis is on the meaning and on reprogramming the mind. That approach is closer to the practice of affirmations than mantras, though.

Over many centuries, the Yogic and Tantric traditions have discovered and developed several wonderful mantras for all sorts of positive effects in our lives, including boosting confidence and courage. As this topic can get rather complex and esoteric and also go to places that may not match the worldview of many of my readers, here I will share only two simple mantras. They are *Ram* and *Hum*, and they are both connected to the solar plexus "energy center" in the body, known as the *manipura chakra* (see Appendix 1). A third mantra that is powerful for self-confidence is *Om Hum Hum Hum Hanumate Phat*. For me this is the most effective of the three, but you may find that another one works better for you.

Please note that according to the Yoga tradition, one should not practice any of these mantras during pregnancy or if one has high blood pressure or inflammatory conditions.

Here are the instructions for mantra meditation:

1. Sit in a meditation posture. Close your eyes.

2. Begin whispering one of these three mantras continuously. You can sync it with your breath if you like, but that is not required (I personally don't).

3. Keep a steady rhythm, be it fast or slow.

4. Just as with affirmation practice, repeat the mantra with concentration, willpower, faith, and feeling. If any of these is missing, the practice will feel empty and tedious.

5. With every utterance, imagine that the mantra is striking and *activating* the solar plexus, which is located behind the navel. To keep your mind focused on that center, you can also imagine that the sound is coming from there. Feel strength, groundedness, courage, and energy developing inside of you with each repetition.

6. Alternatively, you can develop the feeling of surrendering yourself to the mantra, and allow it to fill your whole body. Connect your mind to the vibration of the mantra. Become one with it.

7. When you are done, stop the mantra and focus on the solar plexus for two minutes.

8. Repeat your resolution (*sankalpa*) to yourself three times, and conclude the meditation.

The "minimum dosage" for this practice to be effective, based on the guidelines from my teachers and my own experience, is fifteen minutes. You can start with five minutes, and gradually build up to fifteen. For best results, aim to grow it to twenty-four minutes.

The effect of this practice is often subtle. If you have good concentration and sensitivity and are using a mantra that matches you well, you could experience some results from the very first session. In most cases, however, it is better not to expect that. The mantra is not a magic pill, but a vibration that slowly transforms your mind from within as you keep up with the daily practice over weeks and months. My advice, as a meditation teacher, is to have patience with the process. Try this technique daily for at least ten consecutive days—or longer if your concentration is poor—before deciding whether it works for you.

Of course, if you don't believe that mantras can work, then don't try this practice, as you can't start the process with doubt and expect to end it with confidence. So if you are skeptical about the power of mantras, you can instead use the other meditation techniques in this book.

A note about the third mantra I mentioned: it is a mantra connected to Hanuman, a warrior deity in the Hindu pantheon. If that is a problem for you due to your religious or philosophical inclinations, then don't use that particular mantra, and use one of the other two mantras instead. One way of reading such practice is thinking that Hanuman is a real entity somewhere in the universe, and that by chanting the mantra we are connecting ourselves with him energetically and partaking of his strengths. That is how they see it in India. Another way of approaching this practice is that Hanuman is simply a symbol of certain virtues, an archetype of the perfect warrior spirit and all the qualities that come with it. This is the interpretation that's most popular in the West. In the long term, these two approaches do lead to different places, but for the sake of increasing your self-confidence and inner power, that difference is not relevant. Work with what makes sense to you.

Box Breathing

Calmness begets confidence, so you need a quick way to bring about calmness in daily life, especially when you are facing challenges. One of the best shortcuts to calmness is breathing exercises. When you breathe calm, slow, and long breaths, you send a clear message to your nervous system that all is well.

For that purpose, you can try an exercise known as Box Breathing, where you breathe in and out through the nose in the following pattern:

- Breathe in for four seconds

- Hold your breath for four seconds

- Breathe out for four seconds

- Hold empty for four seconds

That makes one cycle. Do fifteen to twenty cycles like this, and your mind will be in a different state. It takes only about four minutes, and you can practice it any time, with eyes open or closed.

Your breathing should be slow, relaxed, and even. If a ratio of four seconds is too hard, you can do three seconds; if it's too easy, you can increase the count to five, six, or seven seconds. Finally, in this exercise, don't worry about your thoughts—simply focus on your breathing and the counting.

To enhance this practice, once you are done with the breathing, you can include a quick mindfulness exercise to feel more grounded in the moment. It could be, for example, the 5-4-3-2-1 exercise: notice five things you can see, four things you can touch, three things you can hear, two things you can smell, and one taste in your mouth. Another way would be to simply bring your attention to the soles of your feet, and notice the sensations of your feet touching the ground as you splay your toes.

General Guidelines for All Techniques

- Posture: You can meditate seated on a cushion or a chair. The essential thing about posture is that your spine is fully straight, from the lower back to the neck. Ideally you are not leaning on anything.

- Time: The best time to meditate is usually first thing in the morning, so you don't skip it and so the impact it has on your day is stronger. Having said that, any time that works for you is fine! In any case, it should be a time when you are not exhausted or sleepy, and not immediately after meals.

- Place: Choose a spot where you can sit uninterrupted, ideally a place that is quiet, clean, and tidy. This helps create a more conducive state of mind.

- Length: You can start with as little as three minutes, and increase by one or two minutes per week until you arrive at your ideal session length.

- Preparation: Put your phone on airplane mode during your practice, and make sure nobody will interrupt you. Wear clothes that are comfortable and loose, if circumstances permit. Relax your body with deep breathing exercises before meditation.

The meditation techniques taught in this chapter will help you train your awareness and willpower, and also have a direct effect on your self-confidence. Keeping a daily meditation practice, alongside the ongoing application of your favorite tools from the Awareness Pillar, will support you to overcome the conditioned identity and embody your aspirational identity. Next, let's learn about how you can take concrete action in your life in a way that affirms your confident self.

PART 4

THE ACTION PILLAR
Expressing Confidence

14.

Building Confidence from the Outside In

A good stance and posture reflect a proper state of mind.

—Morihei Ueshiba (founder of Aikido)

Action seems to follow feelings, but really action and feelings go together.
By regulating the action, which is under the more direct control of the will,
we can indirectly regulate the feeling, which is not.

—Dr. William James

Don't fake it till you make it.
Fake it till you become it.

—Amy Cuddy

The way you feel is affected by a myriad of things, from the way you speak, the way you dress, and how you move, to the people around you, the weather, your hormones, the type of music you listen to, and even the colors of your room. Some of these factors you have little to no control over; others you can change so they support you to feel your best. Think of them as confidence boosters, as surrounding yourself with confidence triggers so the inner work happens more easily.

Body and mind are tightly connected. Not only does your mind affect your body, but your body also affects your mind—a concept we partially explored in the embodiment chapter.

This latter approach is extremely popular in the personal growth movement. You may ask, "Giovanni, isn't that superficial and not aligned with the deeper approach of living inside out?" It depends. If the "outside-in methods" are used as an aid in *expressing* your new identity, then it can be a support to you living that identity, while the rest of your personality is still catching up. But if that underlying work is not there, then it's often just a Band-Aid solution—attempting to press the "confidence buttons" from the outside while inside you sustain a low self-image. Resorting to shortcuts could be the result of laziness about doing the internal work. In any case, the outside-in approaches may not be powerful enough to override loud internal voices of self-doubt and self-loathing.

Can you boost your self-confidence by "dressing to kill," keeping steady eye contact, adopting power poses, and listening to an uplifting playlist before a meeting? Sure. You can create some level of confidence through such means, and at times it might be exactly what you need. Yet if you do these things without doing the internal self-transformation work, your conditioned identity will be constantly pulling you out of it. You can evoke a mood of confidence in the moment by acting the part, but what will happen when that mood wears out? You'll be back at your baseline—your old identity.

If you just focus on the externals, you are living *outside in*. This can easily lead to false confidence, where you act confident on the outside but deep inside you are really full of doubt, fear, and performance anxiety. Some people will see through that. But even if they don't, *you* will. You might be able to fool everybody else, but not yourself. No lasting sense of security or ease can be built on such a foundation.

I had a client who had exactly that challenge. He knew everything there was to know about the body language of confidence, how social cues are interpreted, how to look confident, and how to be charming and charismatic. But he had not yet done the deeper underlying work. As a result, whenever he was with people, he was so busy in his mind overmonitoring all these external factors so he could play the part. It was a deeply anxious situation for him. The result is that he was not confident because he was doing something that confident people never do: worry about how others will perceive you, and being tense in your ways.

Without the underlying self-transformation work, following the tips in this chapter can help you display enough confidence to pass by in life, but it won't be deep nor effortless nor stable. On the other hand, if you are constantly cultivating your aspirational identity, shifting into it with the tools covered in the first two pillars, then using the tips in this chapter will nicely support you to show up as who you aspire to be.

POSTURE, BODY LANGUAGE, AND APPEARANCE

Your posture and body language affect not only how others feel about you but also how you feel about yourself. The way you sit, stand, and move sends signals to your brain about whether there's a threat in your environment or not.

Stand Confidently

Researcher Amy Cuddy has demonstrated that even two minutes of changing your posture to what she calls a power pose will increase your confidence and reduce stress hormones, such as cortisol, in the body. After doing the power pose, the subjects of her research had higher testosterone levels, were less risk-averse, and did better in job interviews.[1] Other people perceived them as more confident, passionate, authentic, and comfortable.

So what is a power pose? It's a posture in which you spread your body, make yourself big, and intentionally take up more space. You stand up straight, with your shoulders slightly back, feet apart, and arms uncrossed. This is the body language of being calm, open, and expansive.

It tells your nervous system that you are in control and projects that confidence around you.

Be careful not to exaggerate the pose, though. The difference between looking confident and looking cocky is just the angle. Spread your legs a little too wide or puff your chest a little too much, and you'll look pretentious, not confident. Or perhaps even overtly sexual. So be wise about this. On a similar note, make sure that you keep your chin slightly down; otherwise you might look (and feel) arrogant. Combine chin-down with eyes-up, and nobody will misunderstand your calmness for weakness.

The practice of inverted poses in Yoga, as well as the stances of martial arts, can help you naturally adopt more power poses, including in more dynamic ways. Indeed, the power pose applies not only to sitting and standing but also to moving and walking. It's basically a whole new way of being in your body. It's a way of carrying yourself that shows presence, energy, and dignity. Interestingly, it is the opposite of how we typically sit or stand when we are immersed in our phones. That reveals the nature of that state: absence (being disconnected from our environment) and disempowerment (being distracted and stuck in reactive mode).

The opposite of the power pose makes you feel weak and look weak. It is when you are closing in and guarding yourself, with your head hanging, appearing small and fragile. This can happen when you cross your arms in a tense manner and hunch forward. It is interesting to note that by doing that you are closing your core and "protecting" it, likely because you don't feel safe or strong there.

Adopting power poses requires the *awareness* to notice whenever you are physically and emotionally shrinking and the *willpower* to then shift back to confidence. So it takes some self-discipline. As with everything, it might feel awkward in the beginning, but over time it will become second nature.

Move Confidently

Here is an interesting experiment: next time you are out and about, try to guess people's state of mind by how they are walking. You will notice that confident people move differently from insecure and anxious people; that people who are happy and engaged in life walk differently from those who are bored, depressed, or worried. And again, changing your emotions will change how you move, but changing how you move will also help you change your emotions.

So how can you move in a way that produces a more positive and confident state of mind? Walk with purpose. That doesn't mean walking in a hurry or doing a catwalk like a supermodel, but walking with presence, energy, and direction.

Many of the same guidelines for power poses apply here too. You walk with a straight back instead of having a hunched back or your head hanging down. You walk with firm and well-paced steps instead of shy and slow steps. Your feet are not too close together, as if you are afraid of taking space. You're not hiding behind other people, nor are you walking lifelessly. You move freely, with dignity and purpose. There is an openness and relaxation about it, but also a sense of strength and groundedness. And it's better to not walk with your hands in your pockets—that may make you look fragile or somewhat suspicious.

When interacting with others, look people in the eye, but without staring. A good guideline is to hold firm but gentle eye contact for two seconds longer than you'd feel comfortable. The practice of Trataka meditation, especially on a candle flame or a mirror reflection (see chapter 13), will help you feel more comfortable about maintaining eye contact. It will also give you more mesmerizing eyes.

Look Confident

The trillion-dollar fashion and makeup industry is evidence of the human thirst to feel good by dressing well and feel confident by looking confident. "Dress the way you want to feel," they say. It can help express the new self-image you are cultivating. For the same reason, taking care of your appearance via grooming, a nice haircut, good personal hygiene, and good smell can also affect how you feel.

The link between how you dress and how you feel, although real, is not as strong as the link between your emotions and body dynamics. I know I could go outside in my pajamas, with disheveled hair, and still feel confident (albeit awkward). On the other hand, I'm not sure I could spend a whole day sitting and moving like a depressed person without that affecting how I feel.

You can get to a point, through inner work, where you could dress in anything, move in any way, be in any posture, and still feel confident— because there is a fire burning inside of you that cannot be ignored. Until that happens, comb your hair, dress in style, stand powerfully, and speak with energy.

Physical Exercise

Taking care of your body through regular physical exercise has multiple benefits for self-confidence, being both an *outside-in* and *inside-out* approach. Exercise changes your body and the way you feel about your body. It gives you a sense of efficacy, skill, and resilience in overcoming challenges, as well as the taste for success and accomplishment. You feel that if you can take baby steps and improve in this area of your life, you'll likely be able to do the same in other areas of life. Finally, physical exercise helps you increase your willpower and vitality, both of which help you feel more capable in life.

While exercise is not an essential piece to the framework of this book, it is something that can greatly aid your journey to self-confidence, and I encourage you to explore forms of physical exercise that can help you experience the aforementioned benefits.

SPEAK CONFIDENTLY

Just as with your body posture, movements, and appearance, your voice and speaking habits affect how others perceive you and how you perceive yourself. Speaking is one of the main forms of self-expression. The features of your voice—volume, speed, depth, tonality—and the actual things you say tell a story about who you are.

Here is my question for you: Are the words you use and the way you speak making you feel more positive and empowered, or are they confirming your conditioned identity? Are they highlighting your value to those around you or reinforcing a poor image? Think about it. How do you speak when you feel confident? How would your aspirational identity speak? Assertively and purposefully. There is a calm certainty behind what you say.

Conversely, when you're talking from a place of low self-confidence or low self-esteem, you speak hesitantly, don't project your voice, and don't put energy or intention behind your words. You tend to apologize for everything, which makes you feel that you are a constant bother, and sends out the message that you make a lot of mistakes.

Here are some guidelines that are in line with shifting from outside in. You can practice these to start producing, to some degree, the underlying state of confidence via your speech.

- Talk less. If you talk too much or talk all the time, your words have less power, and your mind gets more agitated. Both these things affect how much inner power you have. When you speak less, it's also easier to practice awareness. You have more time to breathe, you can think before you speak, and you sound more thoughtful.

- Talk purposefully. Put some energy and intention behind every word you say. Talk with the conviction that your point of view matters. Breathe life into your words and feel their meaning. Of course, you won't be able to do this every time, but practice it a little bit every day and notice how you sound different, and feel different.

- Speak loudly and clearly. When you come from a place of confidence, you're not afraid to own your voice. You speak because you have something to say. Your goal is to be heard, not just to say things. If you naturally have a low tone of voice or tend to mumble, try this little trick: imagine that your listener is standing three feet farther away from you than they actually are.

- Speak unhurriedly. When you speak too fast, you're sending a message of nervousness, insecurity, and agitation. You are assuming that your listeners won't pay attention and that you need to get the message out quickly before they stop listening. Your voice and words thus lose power. Instead, pause more and slow down.

- Speak assertively. Stand behind your words. Don't downplay what you say by adding "I guess," "Who knows!" "Kinda," or "I'll try." Don't make every sentence sound like a question by ending it with a high intonation. And if you make a request, ask it with the feeling that you really want it to be respected and expect it to be so.

Remember that all of the principles of Wise Confidence outlined in chapter 1 apply here. Your voice is your power, so use it responsibly and kindly. It's not about speaking in a dominant way, but in an empowered way. It's not about persuasion, but about presence and energy. You don't need to control others, but you don't need to apologize for your existence either.

15.

Live Courageously

If you hear a voice inside of you say that you cannot paint,
then by all means paint, and that voice will be silenced.

—attributed to Vincent Van Gogh

Stay afraid, but do it anyway. What's important is the action.
You don't have to wait to be confident.
Just do it and eventually the confidence will follow.

—Carrie Fisher

The world doesn't get less scary. You just get more brave.

—Jordan Peterson

O ne of the main expressions of confidence is courage. Confident people have more courage to face challenges, and by practicing facing challenges you can also develop more courage and confidence. It's a two-way street. So, when you practice *living inside out*, you show up with the courage you would have if you had already fully integrated your aspirational identity. You do so gradually, with proper preparation and tools to help you deal with any setbacks or painful emotions that may arise.

Courage is our ability to act in spite of fear. Fear is our emotional response to a perceived threat, be it real or imagined. It's a survival mechanism that pushes us to fight, flight, or freeze whenever there is a possibility of harm. This can be a functional pattern when we are facing real danger, but it is crippling when applied to the wrong circumstances. If fear becomes your way of being, your core narrative—the lens through which you see the world—then you end up fearing things you shouldn't trouble fearing or fearing things just because they are unknown.

Most people have fear of the unknown as a constant background noise in their minds, often without being aware of it. Why do we fear the unknown? Because it's uncertain. You don't know what's in there. You don't know what's going to happen, so you feel unsafe. In truth, there is nothing scary about the unknown, but the monkey mind will project scary things onto it. You can look at uncertainty as a dangerous territory that should be treaded conservatively, or you can look at it as an exciting field of possibility. One of these thoughts leads to fear and the other to courage. Why do we choose the one we choose? Because of our identity.

The more fragile you are, the more you fear. The stronger you are, the less you need to fear. The difference between being fragile or being strong is not in your muscles, intelligence, or financial resources. It is in your mind. It depends on how you see yourself—your identity or self-image. If you perceive yourself strong, you will be brave, for you know that you can deal with challenges effectively. And if you have the solid *determination* that no matter what happens you shall not break, then you will experience true inner power and freedom.

Nothing exciting can happen in our lives if we constantly avoid the unknown. We cannot express our full potential, try new things, or take meaningful risks this way. Fulfillment will elude us. So will peace, power, and purpose. Yes, developing self-confidence—and the courage that comes with it—is *that* important. But our society is not going to help us with this.

RECOGNIZING OUR CULTURE OF FEAR

We are living in the most fearmongering time in human history.
And the main reason for this is that there's a lot of power and money
available to individuals and organizations who can perpetuate these fears.

—Barry Glassner

There no longer seems to be anything that is really secure.
We seem to be obsessed with every conceivable danger.
Fear has become a basic characteristic of our entire culture.

—Lars Svendsen

Modern culture promotes fear in many ways. On the news and every-where in social media, we constantly hear about threats and dangers, about things that can go wrong, about other people's fails. There seems to be a never-ending list of things we need to keep in mind so we don't eat the wrong thing, say the wrong word, parent the wrong way, or breathe the wrong air. This perspective of fear is so ingrained in our society that we feel it is normal, and we are unaware of how it is influencing our minds and behavior. If we dare to try something that is considered risky by any safety regulations, however conservative, we are shamed.

As a result, it's easy for us to become obsessed with risk aversion. This is not a good thing. Our brain is plastic, and our consciousness can take on any form. Our mind takes on the shape of what it dwells upon repeat-edly. If we are constantly thinking about what could go wrong—the risks, dangers, and failures—then naturally our mind will be full of fear, anxiety, and a sense of powerlessness. If, instead, we focus on *possibility*, on our values and aspirations, on what could go *right*, then we will take more positive action in life, which increases our chances of experiencing positive outcomes. Even if every positive outcome doesn't happen, it's still a more fulfilling and purposeful way to live.

Life has always had uncertainty built in. In centuries past, that uncer-tainty was balanced by hope, optimism, and faith. We didn't emphasize human fragility as we do today, but rather human *potential*. A dose of risk, danger, and pain was seen as normal in any undertaking. "Fortune favors the brave" says the Greek proverb. But in the last decades we began to change our relationship to uncertainty and fear. To learn more about how and why this happened, I recommend you read *How Fear Works: Culture of Fear in the Twenty-First Century* by Frank Furedi. My point here is just to raise awareness of the fact that our modern culture is not raising empowered, wise, and courageous individuals. If you want any of that, then you'll need to find it within yourself, and *live inside out* from that place.

If you overemphasize the value of security, then you'll choose safety and caution whenever facing any amount of risk or uncertainty. Doing so reinforces an identity of fear and low self-confidence. You are limiting your freedom to explore. You are telling yourself that you don't have the strength and maturity to deal with challenges. It's another example of how living *outside in* enhances our insecurities.

It's unwise to take meaningless risks, but it's also unwise to avoid every risk. Life is uncertain, and the world can indeed be a dangerous place. But you have a choice of how you want to navigate it. You can rely on your fears, or you can rely on your strengths. These are two very different ways of living, and only one of them leads to confidence.

HOW TO FACE YOUR FEARS

Here's something to remember:
Actions feed and strengthen confidence; inaction in all forms feeds fear.
To fight fear, act. To increase fear—wait, put off, postpone.

—David Schwartz

You gain strength, courage, and confidence by every experience
in which you really stop to look fear in the face.

—Eleanor Roosevelt

Do the thing you fear and the death of fear is certain.

—Ralph Waldo Emerson

To live with confidence and the courage it engenders, we need to face our fears consistently. Every time we face a fear we weaken it, because we see the feared object for what it is, and it's almost never as terrifying as we thought.

Facing our fears means stretching ourselves beyond our comfort zone. This, in turn, increases our belief in our capacity, and self-esteem. We learn, from experience, that we can handle much more than we originally thought.

Paradoxically, going beyond your comfort zone eventually makes your life *more comfortable*. In the short term you experience some discomfort, for sure. But when you learn to release resistance toward unpleasant emotions, thus widening your capacity, what was once uncomfortable begins to feel like nothing. By stretching your comfort zone every day, you gain the ability to feel comfortable and confident in a wide variety of situations.

If you are unwilling to do that, you can never develop true confidence. You'll be looking for tips and tricks and using them as crutches. You will avoid taking risks so you can remain in the only place where you feel okay: your comfort zone. For example, you sit at the back of the conference room to avoid interactions, arrive late for meetings to avoid small talk, never go anywhere alone, or overprepare for everything. Those are known as safety behaviors in psychology. They may work in the short-term, but they often end up hurting your confidence in the long-term.

The way to go from comfort zone to confidence is by regularly practicing *exposure therapy*, also known as systematic desensitization. In this method, you expose yourself to the feared event little by little, in real life or through visualization, in a way that feels uncomfortable but not overwhelming. While going through the experience, you manage your emotions through deep breathing, relaxation techniques, and awareness tools.

The reason this method works is because the amygdala—aka your "lizard brain"—only learns when you are afraid. So by gradually exposing yourself to fear triggers, you have the opportunity to retrain your lizard brain to feel different about them. As you repeatedly expose yourself to the things you fear, you become desensitized to that stimuli. It begins to feel normal, rather than threatening. What was unknown and unbearable becomes known and bearable. There is no longer a reason to fear.

If you face a big fear all at once, the experience may be overwhelming and even traumatizing. On the other hand, if you avoid facing the fear altogether, you are bowing to it and letting it impose limits in your life. The practical way forward is exposure therapy. It allows you to rewire deep-seated beliefs about what you can and cannot do, and it does so at a very deep layer.

After some time and regular practice, you begin to feel that no matter what happens, you'll be okay. You know that you might experience difficult emotions as a result of trying things that stretch you, but you have learned to accept them, and you know you have the capacity to manage them. That type of courage, self-belief, and optimism are essential ingredients of Wise Confidence.

Let's now see how you can effectively implement exposure therapy to live with more courage and confidence.

Step 1: List Opportunities

Where in your life is fear or anxiety holding you back? If you were perfectly grounded in confidence, what things would you do that you are currently not exploring? Make a list. Let this list be as complete and ambitious as you want. Temporarily suspend the voice of self-doubt which says, "That would be great, but I'll never be able to do it."

Your items may be grandiose, basic, or anywhere in between. It's all good. If it is something that stretches you out of your comfort zone, however simple, it is good for exposure therapy. Here are some ideas, of varying levels of difficulty:

- Ask a question in your next meeting.

- Go to the movies by yourself.

- Start a conversation with a stranger every day.

- Take a 30-day rejection challenge, where you aim to get one "no" every day.

- Take a class in something you have never done before.

- Make a silly "mistake" in public, such as spilling your drink, and then calmly clean it up as if nothing happened.

- Tell a co-worker of a small personal failure you had.

- Ask someone on a date who you think is "out of your league," and do so with the conviction that you will get a yes.

- Tell a joke or a story in a group setting.

- Challenge a stranger to a round of Rock, Paper, Scissors.

- Cheer loudly at a sports event.

- Request a 10 percent discount the next time you order coffee.

- Give someone a compliment.

- Spend a day outside without your phone.

- State your sincere opinion on a topic that matters, even though you know others might disagree with you.

Step 2: Make a Plan

At this point you have a list of things you feel scared of doing—great! Now sort them in order of difficulty, so you know where to start. I suggest you create three categories:

- Easy. On the top of the list, put things you could do now by facing a minimum amount of discomfort.

- Medium. Next, list the things that would cause you some emotional distress, but that on a good day, with strong intention, you could stomach.

- Hard. At the bottom, include the things that you're just not willing to do yet.

Start by doing exposure therapy with the items in the easy category. Once you finish those, or if you are up for a challenge, you can tackle some items from the medium category. As for the items in the hard category, you don't tackle them directly, but break them down into smaller steps or sub-tasks so they fall in the easy or medium category. In this way you slowly train yourself to overcome big fears.

The challenge you pick needs to be big enough so it stretches you, but not so big that it paralyzes you. The sweet spot is when you feel the fear but are capable of acting anyway, with a little push. As you practice this, your fear threshold will get higher and higher, and you won't be so easily triggered anymore.

For example, if you need to overcome a fear of heights, your plan could be to start by slowly exposing yourself to being in enclosed high places, like an apartment building. Then you would progress to looking down through the window, first from the first floor and later on from higher floors. After that you could try being in an elevated open-air location, like a hot air balloon. Eventually you can even try bungee jumping and sky diving. The same approach applies for overcoming fear of rejection, fear of public speaking, fear of failure, and most other fears.

Go gradually, so you experience one small success after another without traumatizing yourself with overwhelming experiences. Step by step, you become more confident and ready for bigger challenges.

Step 3: Develop the Right Mindset

It's important that you understand the purpose of exposure therapy and what you can expect from the process.

First, expect some level of emotional discomfort or even distress. That is a sign that you are going beyond your comfort zone. If you don't feel discomfort, it's because you are not stretching yourself enough— then you are not building confidence nor courage. You might experience rejection, feel silly, be ignored, or get mocked. Learning how to feel comfortable with these experiences is part of the exercise, as it's how you will liberate yourself from the grip of fear.

Second, remember that you are in control here. Since the failures and rejections you will experience are *intentional* and highly expected, they say nothing about who you are. You can actually be grateful for these experiences, as they provide you an opportunity to practice and grow.

Third, know that overcoming your fears takes some time, commitment, and willpower. It takes willingness to do the emotional work. It takes consistence and perseverance, as you need to practice it frequently to get the desired results. But once you get the taste of growth and expansion, you will feel that it was all worth it.

Step 4: Exposure via Imagination

Once you have your list of exposure therapy ideas, know what you want to try first, and have the right mindset about it, then it's time to get started. There are two ways to go about it: you can either visualize yourself going through that situation (step 4), or you can actually go through it (step 5).

To do exposure therapy via imagination, use the POWER Visualization explained in chapter 8. This exercise trains your brain to manage the bodily sensations of fear, anxiety, or shame that may come up. You can use it as a stepping stone toward exposure therapy in real life. If the challenge you wish to tackle is a bit too difficult right now, you may want to go through it a few times in your mind before facing it in the real world. You can also use it for cases in which it is not possible or not desirable to go through the actual situation.

Step 5: Exposure in Real Life

This is the final part of the process: go and actually do the thing you fear, and experience the emotions. Your heart may palpitate, your body may shiver, your stomach may contract. These are good signs; they show that the exercise is working. Feel the sensations, but don't let them stop you. Stay there with acceptance and determination. Tell yourself this is just an experiment and you want to see what happens.

If you like, and the situation allows, you could also use the ROAR Method (chapter 10) to manage your emotions, or use any other techniques from the Awareness Pillar. This gives you the confidence you need to deal with difficult emotions when they arise. With that realization you can live a bigger life, since now you don't need to avoid things just because they make you uncomfortable. You will have trained yourself to be at ease even in the midst of unpleasant emotions. Anxiety and fear won't be able to stop you anymore.

It's important that you stay in the feared situation long enough for your fear to subside. That's the point where you can say, "I did it!" If, instead, you leave as soon as you begin to feel uncomfortable, you would be reinforcing a sense of helplessness in relation to your fears, which would further damage your confidence.

You may need to repeat a particular exposure therapy exercise multiple times until you feel an activity no longer triggers you. At that point, congratulations! Celebrate your win, and get ready to move on to the next item on your list.

ACT DESPITE FEAR

Living courageously is about knowing what you want in life and taking consistent action toward it, even in the face of fear, anxiety, or self-doubt. Feel the fear and do it anyway. Feel the doubt and act as if it doesn't exist. This is both expression of and a training for self-confidence.

"But, Giovanni, taking action when I'm afraid is not easy." If it were, everybody would be confident, which is not the case. This book doesn't promise you an easy path. It promises you a *clear* path and effective tools. An easy path leads to superficial results; real self-transformation takes effort and perseverance. Always.

Fear can be the occasional background noise of a life of confidence. You don't expect fear not to be there so you can act. Rather, you have the confidence that fear cannot stop you. As a result, you experience more freedom in your life. You set goals that scare you, goals that are outside your comfort zone, goals that will really move the needle for you. You don't coast.

What is the point of living under fear? You are *not* going to survive this life. No one will. But in the time that you are here, in this body, you have a choice: to live quietly, afraid of taking risks, and making sure you don't bother anybody; or to live boldly, pursue your dreams, and make some noise. It's not about throwing caution to the wind and being reckless—that is not Wise Confidence. It's about being so charged with your purpose, that fear stands no chance. If something is aligned with your purpose and authentic to your being, then do it. Fear is irrelevant.

Where in your life are you feeling stuck? What is the next action you need to take to get unstuck? Identify it, break it down into baby steps, then take action. Make that big move you know you need to make but have been fearing. Do whatever is needed to move forward.

Action is the ultimate confirmation of belief. Taking consistent action forward will build your confidence. It takes you from being stuck to being in movement. It's an expression of your commitment to live from your aspirational identity, rather than your conditioned identity. Imagine the confidence you will have once you have fully embodied your aspirational identity. Act with *that* confidence.

16.

Improve Continuously

Everything is hard before it is easy.

—attributed to Goethe

The man who does not read has no advantage
over the man who cannot read.

—Unknown

In the beginning of this book, we saw how confidence and competence are two different things. We learned that competence is your skill in a certain field, while confidence is a combination of self-belief, courage, optimism, integrity, and willpower. Confidence is, in a way, more important than competence, for it maximizes your existing skills; and if you lack it completely you won't be able to effectively use your skills. If no amount of skill will ever be enough for you to feel confident, then working on new competencies won't help—you need the internal work of upgrading your self-image.

Having said that, competence is also extremely important. It doesn't replace the need for confidence, but it makes it easier to develop. It's not a requirement for self-confidence, but a training ground for it. Why?

Because you will face several challenges on the path of learning any skill—be it music, a sport, a craft, a foreign language, people skills, or emotional regulation, to name a few. At many points you may feel you are not good at it, you may make excuses and want to give up, or you may procrastinate on doing the work. Every time you face and successfully overcome an obstacle like that, you build greater self-confidence.

This book has covered many ways to feel more confident and live *inside out* from your aspirational identity. It's now time to put it to practice. In the previous chapter we explored how to do this by facing your fears; in this chapter, we'll talk about using the process of learning skills as a training for self-confidence—something that will help you put into practice what you've learned so far.

WHAT TO FOCUS ON

There is an infinite number of things you can learn, but it's impossible to pursue them all. So, which one should you choose? For the purpose of developing confidence, it doesn't matter much. Any skill that you desire to learn and that stretches you beyond your current capacity will do. The more difficult that skill is for you, the deeper and more fulfilling the training will be.

If you are feeling ambitious, pick something that you think you could never do. Maybe it's dancing, public speaking, or rock climbing. By working on a challenging skill and persevering, you are teaching yourself that you can do things even if your mind tells you that you can't. You'll be surprised by what you can achieve! Then you can use this opportunity to transfer this newly found confidence to your whole personality—transforming experiences of self-efficacy into a pervasive sense of self-belief.

Another way of thinking about choosing what to learn is to first look at your values, aspirations, and goals. What are the most important habits and skills that you need to make progress? What skills does your aspirational identity have that you don't yet? Remember, virtues and personal qualities are also skills that can be learned, so consider those too. Identify the relevant gaps and focus on the one or two things that will move the needle the most for you. Once you have achieved the desired proficiency, then you can either move on to other skills or choose one to pursue lifelong, for mastery.

There are also skills that are essential for everybody, regardless of their career path or lifestyle. These include things like technology skills, effective communication, self-regulation, organization, empathy, problem-solving, and financial literacy. If you lack any of these skills, then picking them up will not only build your confidence but also noticeably improve your quality of life.

Every new skill learned is a new world that opens for you. It expands your life. It also brings you a sense of purpose, excitement, and focus. Have fun exploring new worlds!

HOW TO APPROACH LEARNING

Once you have decided on the next one or two skills you want to learn or improve, it's crucial that you approach the learning process with a growth mindset. Assume that you can actually get good at this thing. Otherwise, the experience might actually hurt your confidence, feeding an existing sense of not being good enough—your conditioned identity.

Approach learning with patience. Go little by little, first tackling challenges that are just a bit outside of your comfort zone (your current capacity) and those you can overcome with some effort and self-discipline. Then gradually grow from there.

Make sure to also cultivate the empowering mindsets covered in chapter 9, such as running an experiment, being kind to yourself, and having realistic expectations. If you need to face fears in the learning process, follow the guidelines for exposure therapy explained in the previous chapter.

Know that it will feel difficult and uncomfortable at times. If it doesn't, it's because you are playing it safe and not stretching yourself, which defeats the purpose of using learning as a training ground for self-confidence. Instead, expect challenges, and face them with the confidence that is part of your aspirational identity. If you fail badly, take time to rest and recover; then get back on track.

Learning requires self-discipline, and thus, it *trains* self-discipline. We can say that self-discipline is the ultimate skill, the meta skill needed to learn any other skill. The more you develop it, the more you'll expand your capacity and believe in yourself.

Finally, consider adding a greater sense of purpose to your learning process by linking it to a cause or aspiration that's greater than yourself. Serve others using your unique skills, whether they are innate or acquired. Being of service to others will increase not only your sense of confidence but also your sense of meaning and value as you focus more on human connection. The impact you make on the people you help will show you that you have something valuable to offer the world—and, therefore, that *you* are valuable.

17.

Relate Authentically

In the path, keep the company of those who are like you or higher.
There is no place for the company of fools.

—attributed to The Buddha

The way you relate to others is an expression of how you relate to yourself (your self-image). You unconsciously send signals to people around you—through your voice, appearance, body language, and words—telling them who you are and how they should see you. In a way, you are training people how to treat you.

It might be hard to accept this truth. It might have been uncomfortable for you to read that sentence, perhaps to the point where you might want to close the book. But if you are ready to take full ownership for your life, that sentence can lead you to an empowering insight.

When you come from a place of high self-esteem and confidence, you relate to people differently than if you come from a place of not being good enough and not believing in yourself. And people will relate to you differently, too. As with feelings, actions, and body language, changing the way you relate with people—and changing the people you choose to keep in your life—is not only an *expression* of your underlying beliefs but also an avenue to change them. It's a two-way street.

The practice of relating with authenticity and empowerment includes two things: changing the people you choose to have in your life and changing the way you show up in those relationships.

Mindset, emotions, and ideas are contagious. So you want to make sure you only have people in your life who reinforce your strengths, believe in you, and help you be the best version of yourself. You want people who instigate positive habits in you and strengthen your self-confidence. On the flip side, you want to "unsubscribe" from friendships, relationships, and influences that simply reinforce your conditioned identity, constantly pulling you back to your old self. Making a radical shift in identity will likely not be welcomed by them—so if you want to be authentic, there is no other way but to let them go. We'll cover this more in step 1 below.

The second aspect of this work comes from the fact that the way you relate with people *itself* can reinforce self-doubt or self-confidence. Allowing people to be in your life who disrespect you, treat you poorly, manipulate you, or excessively criticize you, sends a message to your subconscious mind that you don't have much value. This weakens your confidence, willpower, and motivation. Living this way actively trains you to *lack* confidence and keeps you chained to your conditioned self. We cover strategies for overcoming this challenge in steps 2 and 3 below.

In contrast, when you learn to set boundaries, speak assertively, hold your ground, and remove toxic people from your life, you are sending a powerful message to yourself. You are telling yourself that you are worthy, that your needs and opinions matter, and that you deserve better. People around you then also begin to feel the same.

STEP 1: REVIEW YOUR INFLUENCERS[1]

Are the people in your life feeding your self-confidence or your self-doubt? Are the things you read and watch (books, blogs, news, videos, movies, and social media) feeding your self-confidence or your self-doubt?

We are profoundly influenced by the people we spend time with. Several studies in social sciences show how much we affect each other, both consciously and unconsciously. There is deeply ingrained programming in our brain to conform with social standards so we can be accepted, fit in with society, and thus increase our likelihood of survival. For that purpose, we tend to adopt the same narratives, preferences, biases, habits, and goals as the people we associate ourselves with, because they are seen as the norm. We also tend to care a lot about what our peers think of us, and we're often willing to alter our behavior so that we improve the opinions we think they have. All of this involves *living outside in*. It often comes at the cost of sacrificing your authenticity and personal values.

Given that there is a strong gravity pulling us to become like the people we associate ourselves with, it is wise to choose those people very carefully. This applies not only to your circle of close friends but to everyone you spend time with, learn from, watch, and listen to. Everyone who can plant an idea in your mind or influence your moods in any way is your *influencer*.

If you spend time with people who are anxious, demotivated, and loaded with self-criticism, you will tend to feel, unconsciously, that this is normal and okay. If your partner doesn't believe in you, you will tend to experience self-doubt as well. If the news and movies you watch are all about violence and disaster, they will stimulate the part of you that lives from fear. If most of the information you consume is junk, your mind will be full of junk.

On the other hand, if you spend time with people who are optimistic, you tend to become more optimistic. If most of your friends take meaningful risks in their lives, you will be inspired to do the same. If your partner encourages your dreams, you'll naturally feel more confident to take steps toward them. If the blogs and books you read are uplifting, you will be uplifted. If your colleagues work with care and discipline, you are more likely to do the same.

Here is the key takeaway: Surround yourself with people, books, mentors, and ideas that affirm your aspirational identity. Be around those who have the Power Words you are cultivating and also those who express the archetypes you want to grow into.

The Pitfall of Social Media

As is documented in several research papers, and the experience of many of us, social media can damage our self-confidence and self-esteem.[2] As you scroll through your favorite app, you'll likely find yourself comparing your appearance, your income, your children, your intelligence, or your achievements to the unrealistic and highly curated version of other people's lives.

Another problem is that the way we use social media these days, as conditioned by the way the apps are built, is a tool of unawareness. The social apps are built to keep you hooked, to keep you consuming. They make money when you click, not when you pause and think. As a result, we are consuming information so fast that we don't have time to be aware.

Before you can begin to realize the effect that a certain image or video has had on you, you've already scrolled to the next one. Before you have the time to reflect on if what you just consumed is true or not, helpful or not, aligned with your values or not, you've already gone and hit the next dopamine button. This means that all these influences are entering your subconscious mind without much of a filter. They are creating a new conditioned identity, while you think you're just having fun.

In this manner, the use of social media is stimulating unhealthy comparisons, envy, distraction, and self-obsession. It is influencing you in ways you probably can't imagine and changing your values without you even noticing. It is keeping you hooked, addicted to the ephemeral sense of satisfaction that comes from getting likes, hearts, and followers. It is also wasting a lot of your time and hurting your ability to stay motivated in the pursuit of meaningful goals by getting you accustomed to experiencing rewards effortlessly.

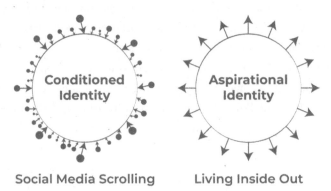

Social Media Scrolling · Living Inside Out

Social media is the worship of junk dopamine. The temple of social validation. The religion of living outside in. If you want to live inside out, it's better to avoid it. If you want to be confident, empowered, focused, and disciplined—have nothing to do with it. There are other ways of staying connected with your friends and getting new information that don't have these drawbacks.

Do you think I'm exaggerating? Then I invite you to run a simple experiment: delete all social media apps from your phone for a month, and don't log in via a web browser either. Notice how that impacts you. Then go back to using them as before, and notice what that does to you.

Is it possible to use social media without any of these negative effects? Maybe, but that is not how these services are programmed, so you'll definitely be swimming against the stream. Very few people have the capacity to use social media in a mindful and empowering way. Even fewer can do that *consistently* without suffering any unintended effects or getting sidetracked. For those who can make that happen, it is not without some constant expenditure of energy, which could arguably be put to better use somewhere else.

Complete abstinence is the most effective approach. If that is not possible for you, then setting strong boundaries via social media fasts and clear rules is your second-best choice. For a detailed explanation on how to do that, check out my other book *Mindful Self-Discipline*.

Exercise: Influencers Inventory

Make an inventory of the influences that are currently operating in your life. List the ten people you spend the most time with, whether you have direct or indirect contact with them. Indirect contact includes the authors you read, websites you regularly visit, videos you watch, and social media accounts you follow.

Then for each one, ask yourself: *How is this person influencing me? While with them, and right after, do I feel negative (agitated, anxious, doubtful, stressed) or positive (calm, empowered, inspired)? Do they make me feel more inclined to follow my aspirations or less so? Do they feed my conditioned self or my aspirational self?*

Once you know the influence each person has in your life, ask yourself: *Do I want more of this, or less of this?* Separate them into three categories: Yes, No, and It's complicated.

- Yes—spend more time with. These are people who feed the best in you, support your growth, inspire you, help you believe in yourself, or encourage you to move toward your aspirations. Keep them close.

- No—spend no time with. These are people with unhealthy life habits, those whose values are not aligned with yours, or those with toxic behaviors. They can be people who undermine your growth, slow you down, and do not really want to see you succeed. Keep them out at all costs, especially if they are toxic. See step 2 below.

- It's complicated—relate wisely. This category encompasses two groups of people: (a) those who have a mix of positive and negative influences on us, and (b) those whose influence we don't like but whose presence we can't or don't want to eliminate from our lives entirely. Perhaps they have good intentions, but become toxic from time to time. You may choose to spend time with them—or you may need to by force of circumstance—but do so wisely, with awareness and strong boundaries. See step 3 below.

It's Not Selfish

Before moving on to steps 2 and 3, let me address one of the most common limiting beliefs around this process: that it is rude or even selfish to cut people out or set limits.

As you grow, become more positive, and strive to live in alignment with your aspirations, you may start losing touch with people whose worldviews are not aligned with your new identity. Some people may be confused or even envious about your newfound strength and boundaries. Don't feel guilty about that. Don't dim your light to accommodate them. You deserve to surround yourself with people who help you shine and be your best.

Some people belong to your past, not your future. Anyone who discourages your positive changes can never be a friend to your aspirational identity. Your aspirational identity would never associate with them in the first place. So choosing to have them in your life or not is a deeper choice—it's a choice about who you want to be.

Spending time with these types of people will make your self-confidence journey harder, so avoid them as much as possible. Life is too short to spend your energy listening to haters, naysayers, narcissists, and fools. Seek the company of those who push you forward. Those who celebrate your success. Those who help you become more of your aspirational self, rather than expect you to stay as your conditioned self.

Don't be afraid to cut ties with people who constantly drag you down or push you in the wrong direction. Doing that is not arrogant nor selfish. It is not that you think you're better than them; it is about having self-respect and setting boundaries. You are simply recognizing that your values and mindsets don't match. This way you respect your own time, well-being, and goals—as well as theirs.

It is worth remembering one of the tenets of this framework: *be wise*. Exposing yourself to *intelligent* criticism from those who have your best interests at heart is healthy. Spending time with *virtuous* people who stretch you and widen your worldview is healthy. Caring for the well-being of those who deeply disagree with you is healthy. Listening to those who make you hate yourself is not. Being in the company of those who discourage your higher values is not. Putting up with toxic influences that drag you down is not.

STEP 2: REMOVE TOXIC PEOPLE

In some cases, a person in our life is not only negative but *toxic*. People who are narcissistic, psychopathic, drama queens, aggressive, manipulative, sadistic, or otherwise unashamedly selfish and uncaring go in this bucket. We need to know how to identify toxic behavior and unapologetically cut it out of our lives. The sooner we do that, the better, so we prevent further damage. Since we can't really expect to change other people, eliminating toxic behavior may mean cutting some people out of our lives entirely.

Some people don't want you to be confident. Either they don't want you to outshine them or they just don't care about you. They are mesmerized by confidence, but they don't want *you* to be confident—at least not more confident than they are. Many will also portray a false image of status, power, or success because they desire to feel above you. There are also people who secretly desire to keep you down, so they don't feel triggered, threatened, or inadequate in your presence. They may even abuse concepts of humility and kindness to keep your confidence in check.

In this section, I use the term *toxic people* knowing that, in essence, there is no clear line separating "good people" and "bad people." We all have some good and some evil inside of us. However, it's precisely this type of thinking and fuzzy boundaries that keep many good people confused and hesitant, and bad people in control. So, although not philosophically precise, the term *toxic*, when applied to people, is pragmatically useful and better than the alternative (lack of clarity).

Toxic people are confidence killers. They try to assert their position in the "dominance hierarchy," and they don't mind if they need to step on you for that. In their own underlying insecurity, they attempt to feel better by placing themselves above you, explicitly or implicitly. They may keep you confused about what is really happening by mixing the good with the bad. For example, at times they will help you or do something that pleases you, but only to the degree that makes you more useful *for them*. They may also praise ideals of cooperation, forgiveness, and acceptance, as long as that applies only to you and not to them. They use these ideas to subtly force you to let them do what they want.

It's likely that you have some people like this in your life—if not, you are almost guaranteed to meet them sooner or later. Perhaps it's your boss, a colleague, a family member, a client, or a friend. How you are treated by them may make you internalize a sense of low self-worth and may create limiting beliefs that prevent you from fully living your values and aspirations. They know how to quickly identify whatever is giving you strength and certainty, then undermine that with distortions, lies, and emotional manipulation. They are experts at their craft and will make you doubt your truth, your insights, and your values.

My decades of living with a narcissist have made me an expert in recognizing emotional manipulation. I can smell it from miles away. And in this section, which could easily be an entire book, I'll share with you my hard-earned insights on this topic and what traps you need to watch out for.

What I share in this section may not apply in total to every toxic person in *your* life. I'm sharing the perspective and the tools to deal with even the most toxic of individuals; use your discernment to apply them in the right dosage, as per the needs of the situation. On another note, you may find that many of these insights are also helpful when setting boundaries with individuals who are only occasionally toxic.

Trap 1: The Shadows of Your Virtues

Virtues are positive character traits that are considered the foundation for living well and a key ingredient of greatness. Virtues are your psychological assets, your personal strengths, your "superpowers." We are talking about things like courage, patience, trust, kindness, confidence, focus, serenity, determination, resilience, and integrity. Cultivating virtues is part of the internal aspect of self-discipline.

Yet it is also true that every virtue casts a shadow. Our greatest strengths, when overused and not balanced, are often the source of our greatest weaknesses. Toxic people are good at spotting and exploiting those weaknesses.

Every virtue is a tool, and we need different tools for different jobs. Don't treat everything as a nail just because you are good with the hammer. You need to develop yourself holistically and pay special attention to cultivating virtues that are opposite to the ones you already have. I call this type of inner work *balancing your virtues*. Until you do this work, the shadow side of your strengths can limit your growth and bring you suffering.

Tolerance is not always the answer—nor is compassion, kindness, acceptance, or forgiveness. We can call all of these the "virtues of niceness," meaning that they are part of being a "nice person." It is good to develop them, and in general the world needs more of them. However, they need to be balanced, so that showing up with these virtues is a *choice*, not a compulsion.

When a toxic person is deliberately invading your space or manipulating you, what you need in that moment is not to be more loving, tolerant, or kind. What you need is the ability to show up with the opposite strengths of assertiveness, justice, and boundaries—otherwise, you become a doormat. And a doormat is not confident, nor powerful, nor happy. A doormat can't make a real impact in the world.

When toxic people know you have these virtues of niceness and lack the ability to set boundaries, they feel in control. They know that if they cross boundaries, you will accept it, that if they are mean, you will tolerate it, and that if they do something wrong, you will forgive them— without their even asking. They know you will continue to be kind. They know this is who you are and that you would hate to be any different. They know you won't try to fully own and display your strengths because you believe that you need to be humble. They know you will not go against them because you are a team player and like to cooperate.

To make things worse, whenever they see you deviating from the virtues of niceness, they will shame you, knowing that you will feel bad about it and take a step back. They'll manipulate you through your shame, which is the shadow side of your goodness. "Good people" are ashamed of being associated with bad behaviors; "bad people" are not ashamed of anything that gives them an advantage.

When you accept the shame projected from others, you are living outside in. Conversely, when you are living *inside out*, nobody can make you feel anything without your permission. They can press your buttons and dump their negativity on you, yes, but they can't make you *feel* negative. You feel solid at your core, and you know you have the power to process those inputs in a way that is aligned with your values and identity.

Tolerance is a virtue that some toxic people manipulate. In life, you will get more of what you tolerate. Toxic people know that fact; good people often don't. Toxic people make use of *your* tolerance to meet their selfish ends, constantly crossing your boundaries to see how far they can go. Nice people without boundaries enable that by accepting even further, in the vain hope that the other person has some of the goodness they project and that they will see how they are in the wrong and will stop.

If something inside of you is nodding and saying "Yes, exactly!" as you read this, then you know how it feels to have toxic people in your life. Now that you are clear about what is really going on, you can begin to turn the tables. You can make yourself immune to toxic people.

How?

First, reject shame. Let nobody make you feel shame. If you avoid that trap, then they can't control you, and they'll soon go bother someone else.

Second, balance your virtues by cultivating the opposite virtues. Become a more complete human being by having the capacity to play the opposite game when the situation calls for it. When fighting demons, don't try to be an angel.

What virtues balance the virtues of niceness? Justice, dignity, self-care, self-protection, self-love, courage, authenticity, boundaries, and assertiveness. These balancing qualities give you the capacity to say a powerful NO to something that is not right or is not aligned with your values. And then stay in that *no* courageously, without budging. Hold your ground as the narcissist repeatedly attempts to shame you for setting boundaries. Know what wrongs you will not tolerate—and then do not tolerate them, come what may.

Humility
Kindness
Tolerance
Politeness
Acceptance
Forgiveness
Compassion

Balancing Virtues

Justice
Self-Care
Toughness
Boundaries
Authenticity
Assertiveness
Self-Protection

Being Nice

Being Strong

If at times you feel like a doormat because you struggle with the shadow side of your virtues, then make sure to include some of the aforementioned "balancing virtues" as your Power Words. You may greatly benefit from awakening the archetype of the warrior in yourself, even though that may be something that never originally attracted you or that you never thought you needed.

Trap 2: Taking on the Wrong Project

Another trap that keeps us disempowered when dealing with toxic people is that we try to change them. It's like we are consciously choosing to have them in our life so we can "help them." The fact is that changing behavior is hard, even when you consciously seek it; if you don't want to change, it'll be impossible.

Toxic people often don't want to change. Why would they? Their behavior is not bothering them; it is bothering you. It seems like *you* have a problem; they don't. Most of them are too in love with the identity that is producing that negative behavior and don't care if that means more suffering for you, as long as they get what they want. Are you sure you want to help them? The more sophisticated ones may pretend the opposite, of course. They'll pretend to care and will do the minimum required for you to maintain that illusion. Don't fall for it. They don't really care. They are using you.

It's not your job to change them. Don't take a toxic person on as a project, as that would be a poor allocation of your precious resources of time and energy. If you want to take on a person as your project, then choose wisely. Choose someone who, with the same amount of effort, attention, and patience, will get much better results. Someone who actually deserves your service and asks for it. Or better, choose *yourself* as the project.

It's not your responsibility to make life easier for everyone around you. Your responsibility is to become the best version of yourself—your aspirational identity—and then to live and serve from that place, according to your values and aspirations.

Trap 3: Fearing the Wrong Thing

The third trap that keeps you hooked to a toxic person—especially if they are a family member or a close friend—is that there is a part of you that is afraid of breaking a bond, being rejected, being misjudged, and ending up alone. They *know* it, and they are using it to buy time. Of course, they will never admit it, even if confronted about it.

When that dynamic is happening, we often focus on the pain we imagine we would feel by cutting them out and ignore the pain we actually feel right now. We are not aware *enough* of all the limitations and negativity brought about by their presence in our life, and the long-term effects of that. If we were, then experiencing their rejection would feel like a low price to pay for our freedom, sanity, and well-being.

Understanding this requires a shift in our thinking. It requires realizing that it is far better to be alone than to be in an abusive relationship of any kind. Loneliness only feels scary when we don't have aspirations to pursue, when we are not engaged with life in a meaningful way. The way to solve that is to find our aspirations and pursue them energetically—rather than accepting the presence of a toxic person for the promise of breadcrumbs of attention.

It is better to experience rejection than to be in an abusive relationship. You shouldn't be worried if a narcissist rejects you; you should be worried if they don't. Because that would mean they see you as an easy target for their manipulative games. It would mean that your conditioned identity is broadcasting signals of fragility, naïveté, and neediness, and they are ready to exploit that. If this is happening for you, know that this is *not* who you really are. You can stop this.

When you live from your empowered self, narcissists will have no interest in you. They will go somewhere else because, through your attitude you have already rejected their way of being. Living inside out is the *best* narcissist repellent!

> *Anything that makes you weak physically,*
> *intellectually, and spiritually, reject it as poison.*
>
> —Swami Vivekananda

A subtler fear that may keep you in a toxic relationship is a fear of being in denial. You worry that what they say about you is right and that it would be irresponsible for you to just close your eyes to it. Toxic people are experts at seeing *your* flaws and terrible at seeing theirs. They are also great at making up flaws in you and convincing you that you have them. They will point them out to you as a way of asserting dominance, but under the guise of helping you become aware and grow. And you—being a good person, a humble person, a growth-oriented person—will listen.

There may be some truth in what they say. That is exactly the challenge. If it were all pure lies and evil, you would probably have already realized it and removed that person from your life long ago. But you get confused because you are looking at those seeds of truth and discounting the rest. This is a trap because they actually don't have your best interests at heart; rather, they are using your virtues against you. Never allow that to happen; otherwise, you might end up resenting your virtues, and that is the path to your downfall.

No matter how nutritious a meal may be, if it has poison mixed in it, don't eat it. Seek your nourishment elsewhere. Let go of the fear that you may not find it. That's what they use to keep you hooked in a toxic relationship.

Your conditioned identity has trouble with boundaries and stays hooked. Your aspirational identity doesn't. Your aspirational identity fears neither rejection nor loneliness—it is strong, authentic, and self-reliant. Live, love, and relate from that place.

Trap 4: Believing Malice Doesn't Exist

Malefic influences need to be removed from your life without hesitation and without looking back. That's what you would do if you were perfectly confident—so if you want to be perfectly confident, do it. I wish I had realized this fact earlier, and I've seen many clients and students struggling with it. That's why I'm not mincing words on this topic.

Malevolence exists. The more you ignore this fact, the more you'll be a victim to it. You stay in relationships with people who are toxic because you don't understand toxicity. It could be because of the shadow sides of your virtues, or because you are taking them on as a "project," or because you are getting some of your needs met and are unwilling to let go of that despite the continuous pain. Whatever the cause, if there are toxic people in your life and you are not wise about it, they will hold you back big time. They'll undermine your confidence and mental health.

I realize that this view is not a popular opinion among meditation teachers and spiritual seekers. I slashed some holy concepts in the mindfulness world, and this may not sound politically correct. I know this may raise eyebrows and make people question how "enlightened" I am. Yet I hold my ground and stay firm on the truths I've seen.

I'm also in good company. There have been many enlightened masters that, contrary to some popular spiritual teachings, believed in setting boundaries and self-defense. Here are some things that my spiritual guru has to say on this topic:

- "In Indian culture there are 33 million gods. Not one of them is without a weapon."

- "We pray for peace, but we are also courageous to stand for ourselves."

- "Gone are the days when someone slaps you in the face and you show the other side to get slapped. Why should we do that? Instead, slap him back three times

so he remembers you for the rest of his life. Evil
people don't understand the language of forgiveness.
They only understand the language of pain."

- "The world needs more *shakti* (empowerment), not
bhakti (devotion)."

In Asia, many Buddhist temples have statues of a fierce "protector spirit" at the entrance—and that is the mythology of a religion that believes in universal goodness and nonviolence! We just cannot afford to be naïve about malevolence and toxicity. Otherwise, we make it difficult for goodness to grow in us and in our society.

If there are no consequences for evil, evil will spread, and good will suffer. If you don't stop it, it won't stop. So defending yourself against unfair treatment is not the enemy of goodness, but the *protector* of goodness. It is not a sin, but a duty. There, I said it.

So yes, I'm a meditation teacher, but one with an uncommon message. I do not emphasize compassion, forgiveness, acceptance, or living in the moment. These *are* important virtues and they have their place, but they are also a delicious feast for evil influences in your life who will stimulate these things in you so they can continue to be at ease as they are. For this and other reasons, in my life and teaching I rather emphasize growth, empowerment, focus, and purpose.

To remove evil from your life, you need two things: clarity and determination. In this chapter I'm doing all I can to help you come to a state of clarity about this. Yet the determination has to come from you. The determination to remove toxicity from your life is a great gift you give yourself, a true act of self-love. Are you ready to make this commitment to yourself?

STEP 3: SET BOUNDARIES

We have talked about what to do with people who should not be in your life at all, but what about the people who may be difficult at times, but whom you still want in your life because they also bring a lot of good things? Or what about toxicity from people whom you, apparently, have no choice but to have in your life? In both cases, it's all about knowing how to set effective boundaries. Actually, you need boundaries even in relationships with people who are generally good for you and who you want to spend more time with.

Much of the resentment we experience in life is related to times when we didn't express ourselves, were not assertive about our needs, or didn't set effective boundaries. A lack of assertive communication can easily lead to regret, hurt, or even abuse. All of this makes it much harder for you to feel confident and empowered. The solution is to master the art of setting boundaries.

Communicate Assertively

There are two main ingredients in assertive communication: clarity and firmness. You say what you want and you want what you say. This is not a license to be rude, blunt, or irresponsible with your words, but it means being unapologetic and unambiguous about your needs. That naturally springs from a heart that knows what it wants and a mind that is unafraid to support that. In other words, it's a natural expression of *living inside out.*

Assertive communication starts with the awareness of your core values and aspirations—which are your personal non-negotiables. When you know yourself and value yourself, you know what you want and are comfortable asking for it. On the other hand, if you don't have clarity about what you want or don't value yourself because of low self-esteem, you'll naturally have poor boundaries and communicate meekly. It is as though you are afraid of existing.

To be more assertive in your communication, first practice saying no. When you really want to say no, say it. There is no need for lengthy explanations. You don't need to justify yourself, as if you are doing something wrong. "No" is a complete sentence. If you want to say no but think you can't, just go ahead and say it. You could say, "Sorry, but I have other commitments," or "I wish I could help you, but I need to stay focused on (passion project/aspiration)," or "Not now, but maybe later," or just "No, thanks."

Second, actually communicate your boundaries. Boundaries will not be respected if they are not communicated. When voicing your boundaries, use clear and unapologetic language. You can use different measurements of strength when expressing them, depending on the personality and cultural background of the other person. Here are some examples that cover varying degrees of intensity and directness:

- I disagree with that.

- That doesn't look fair to me.

- I need a break. Let's continue this conversation later.

- That is not nice. Please don't do it again.

- This is unacceptable.

- You cannot speak to me like this. If you continue, I'll leave the room.

- That's actually not what I asked.

- You are crossing some boundaries here.

- I'm not ready to make a decision right now. I need some time.

- I have my reasons, but I don't need to give you any explanations.

- That's not what we have agreed to.

- This is not my problem. I believe it is yours.

- Yes, I got your email, but it was after hours so I'm only reading it now.

- I'm not happy with that.

- That's offensive!

- No, I won't do that.

- That's a very personal question. Why do you want to know?

- I don't think I have to answer that question.

- You need to lower your voice if you want me to listen.

- I won't play this game.

- What are you suggesting?

- What did you just say?

- That is not going to work for me.

- I see what you are doing. You're trying to manipulate me using shame.

- I'm sorry, but I don't have time for this right now.

- This is not aligned with my values, so I'll have to say no.

The important thing is to not second-guess yourself but to speak with conviction and without diffidence. This requires getting comfortable with being somewhat disagreeable—which is totally fine, because the other party asked for it the moment they stepped on your toes.

How do you know if you are communicating assertively? When you communicate assertively, there is no ambiguity about what you meant. They will know exactly what you are asking for or pushing against. If there is any doubt about it or if they are not taking it seriously, it's likely because the communication was too soft or indirect for them. Turn up the heat a notch or two, and communicate more strongly. Some people just don't get it—so spell it all out for them.

In most cases, it is better to communicate boundaries in a calm and collected manner. If, instead, you communicate with anger and agitation, you may weaken your position and trigger the other person's defense mechanism. It can also show insecurity and a lack of self-control. Some people will exploit that, because they now know which button they can press.

Assertive communication is an aspect of self-confidence. Don't be afraid to use it, but do so wisely. You can be strong and gracious at the same time. People will respect you for it and see you as a mature and empowered individual.

Enforce Your Boundaries

Suppose your boundaries are clear and reasonable and you communicate them assertively, but still they are not respected. What can you do? If you accept that there is nothing you can do and just tolerate it, that will likely eat you up little by little. This is not helpful for your self-confidence or your well-being, and it can also lead to resentment or even trauma.

If you tolerate unfair treatment, you'll get more of it. If you tolerate bullying and disrespect, you'll get more of it. If you tolerate poor life conditions, you won't have the motivation needed to rise above them. Don't give away your power by tolerating what you *need not* tolerate. Such a manifestation of tolerance is not a virtue, but a shadow; not an asset, but a liability.

This reminds me of the story of the boiling frog. If we put a frog in hot water, it will jump out immediately. But if we put it in tepid water and very gradually increase the temperature, the frog will continue to "tolerate it," gradually losing energy until the point where it can no longer tolerate it. Its muscles will become frail, and its spirit, weakened. By then the water will be scalding, and the weary frog won't have the strength needed to jump out. Alas, it gets cooked alive!

If you tolerate toxicity, you may end up like the boiling frog. Instead, respond immediately and strongly, but proportionally. "Kill the monsters when they are young," says the ancient proverb. The response could be a calm but firm verbal rebuke, a formal complaint to an authority, leaving the room, changing the topic, blocking the person on social media, or anything else that feels effective and proportional. Scale your response as the need arises.

One problem is that toxic behavior often catches us off guard, so it can be challenging to respond to it appropriately in the moment. Here is an exercise to train you to respond in a firm and effective manner.

1. Make a table with three columns on a piece of paper or in a digital file.

2. In the first column, make a list of behaviors you are not willing to accept. They could be small things or big things. Think of all the times you were treated unfairly or had your boundaries ignored, and make sure to include all those behaviors.

3. In the second column, rate from one to five how unacceptable each of them is for you.

4. In the third column, write how you will respond to them. It's good to know beforehand exactly what you will do when people push your boundaries; otherwise you might get caught by surprise or freeze in the pressure of the moment and not find the strength to assert yourself.

5. In your daily life, stay connected with yourself and be honest about how you feel in any situation. If you feel that your personal boundaries are being disrespected, in most cases it is better to respond immediately. Let go of any sense of guilt or shame about owning your feelings—asserting your boundaries is *wise*, not selfish.

You may need to be willing to hurt other people's feelings, to some degree, when they are so unaware that they are hurting yours (and others'). Doing so is not mean. It is not selfish. It is compassionate, as it will slowly help them wake up. Otherwise, you are just enabling their selfishness by showing that there are no consequences for their behavior. That does a disservice to you, to them, and to all the future targets of their toxicity.

Get ready to be labeled sensitive, rude, aggressive, uptight, or cold by the offending party. Don't let this type of gaslighting get to you.

Don't let them turn the table. Other people may not get it because they can't psychologically "afford" to get it—they have been that frog in the hot water for far too long, so they insist that you should tolerate it rather than jump out.

Stay grounded in your truth and confident in your response. Don't budge, and you'll be fine. You can say, "I know what you are trying to do here. It's not going to work." That's your confident self speaking! Enjoy its power.

Be Unassailable in Your Spirit

By effort and mindfulness, discipline and self-mastery,
let the wise one make for himself an island
which no flood can overwhelm.

—The Buddha

The more you live *inside out*, the easier setting boundaries becomes. When you do this, you are broadcasting clarity, integrity, confidence, and strength to those around you. When you are not looking outside for validation, you cannot be easily manipulated. There is something in you that cannot be broken, attacked, or shaken. Your values and aspirations are non-negotiable, and your commitment to live them is solid.

There is a story in the Zen tradition that illustrates this point. A Zen master and a monk are walking through a village when a rude and angry person comes and starts insulting the master in all sorts of ways. The master doesn't budge, and the offender eventually leaves, still angry. Later on, the monk asks the master how it is possible that he wasn't moved at all.

"When you buy someone a gift and they don't accept it, to whom does it belong?" the master asked.

"To me," the monk said.

"Likewise with anger," the master said. "If you don't accept the gift, by not feeling offended, it remains with the other person."

I was lucky to learn this lesson early in life, and I used it repeatedly against mockery, verbal abuse, bullying, and condescending jokes. Being unaffected in the midst of offenses is both powerful and peaceful.

Sometimes I would imagine that I was completely empty, like space, and that the other person's toxic words were passing through me and not landing anywhere; or that I was a mirror and their words were just bouncing back to them. At other times, I'd imagine that they were speaking Chinese (a language I don't understand). Or I would—arrogantly but effectively—think of myself as superior to them, like they were ants shouting at a lion. (I don't recommend this third approach anymore, as it is neither wise nor mindful, but if that's the only thing that works for you, then go for it—it's still much better than the alternative of being bullied and broken.)

Once, when I was about nineteen years old, I was dealing with a person in authority who had persistently bullied me and was doing so then. For a change, I decided to try something that a manipulative person would never expect: agreeing with them. I verbally agreed with everything they said, with the same unaffected and light tone of voice, and an emotional distance behind it. With every "I think you're right," they would get even more confused and annoyed. They were hearing a confirmation of their belief, but it was giving zero emotional satisfaction, and they didn't know what to do with that or what to try next. I was pleased that I was finally able to turn the tables, and with so little effort! It taught me an important lesson: that when I refuse to be affected, I'm not giving my power away to the bully.

It is worth repeating: when you are living inside out, nobody can make you feel anything without your permission. While you are in the process of consolidating that mode of being, use whatever metaphor or trick works for you. Be unshakable like a mountain, empty like the sky. This will make you emotionally unassailable and self-reliant. Best of all, this is a technique that, once internalized, requires almost no effort to be maintained.

When you lack confidence, you feel the need to defend yourself, explain yourself, and protect your image. Whatever you do from that space will smell like insecurity—they have triggered you. Instead, defend yourself by being empty. Defend yourself by not needing to defend yourself, and the attack will fall back on the attacker. Just as an empty house cannot be robbed, when you are empty of insecurities you cannot be hurt. You will walk on this earth with uncommon confidence.

Now, do you remember the concept that every virtue casts a shadow? Well, the same is true here. There are two shadows that can come when you apply this approach. I've experienced them both in my life, and have finally come out the other end.

The first shadow is that you may tolerate unfair treatment for far too long. Even if the unfair treatment does not emotionally affect you—because you have mastered the skill of being unassailable—it may affect others around you and have ricochet effects in your life. It's also not fair to allow people to spread their toxicity without consequences, even though *you* might be immune to that poison. As my guru said, toxic people only understand the language of pain, so let us be kind enough to inflict them some—so that they can grow. Or at the very least, they will feel less comfortable about mistreating other people the same way.

The second shadow is that you may become numb to constructive criticism, especially if it is communicated in less-than-skillful ways. Staying grounded in who you are includes having a realistic view of your strengths *and* weaknesses. Such confidence is a useful buffer against internalizing unhelpful criticism or emotional manipulation, but we must be mindful that it doesn't cause us to ignore criticism altogether. That would severely limit our growth in life and also cause difficulties in personal relationships.

Wise Confidence is unassailable, yet it also holds the ability to take in helpful feedback without getting defensive. You need both modes. It's your discernment that will say when it's time to be in unassailable mode or in "Is there truth in this criticism?" mode. When you are truly living inside out, your self-worth is not at risk. This means you can handle criticism, and even rejection, with grace.

DON'T BE NICE. BE POWERFULLY GOOD.

*The only thing necessary for the triumph of evil
is for good men to do nothing.*

—attributed to Edmund Burke

*A person who is not capable of being mean
will be a victim of someone who is.*

—Jordan Peterson

There is a difference between being nice and being good. Being nice is often a coping mechanism. It's an attempt to navigate the world more safely, avoiding conflict because we might not see ourselves as someone strong, as someone who has the right to want something and have an opinion. Being good, on the other hand, is a choice, an aspiration. It is spreading light around you, even when there is no direct payback. Being good comes from an insight that we are all one and that loving your neighbor is like loving yourself. It comes from a loving heart.

Being nice feels good for the other person, but it doesn't necessarily help them. It doesn't make them grow. It just makes them comfortable, and comfort is often the enemy of growth. Instead, be *good*. Have their best interests at heart, and don't be fooled by their displays. That is an expression of love. Love can be nice, but love can also be tough.

Mean people are often very confident. It's "nice people" who are not. In the name of niceness, politeness, and humility, they hold back their power. Niceness should be a secondary value in relation to confidence. When they conflict, choose confidence and authenticity because it is pointless to be nice when it means hurting yourself. That is not sustainable either. The frog will eventually boil.

Confidence is empowerment. It's the prerequisite for you to be able to do good in the world. To be good but powerless is not very useful— you wish us well, but you are not really joining the fight. It doesn't feel that great. The nice-but-powerless people have little impact, and they will be forgotten. The good-and-powerful ones won't.

My bet is that you are a good person; that is why you are looking for a *wise* approach to confidence. And I believe that good people need to be twice as confident as mean people. Otherwise, evil will be powerful and good will be weak, albeit full of compassionate intentions.

Be peaceful and kind, but not weak. This is the concept of *empowered peace*, translated in the image of the meditating lion which I use as a symbol for my work. Empowerment and peace are words not usually seen together because they are considered opposite virtues. This is precisely why I have combined them.

Wise Kindness

The desire to serve, be good, and make a positive impact is a beautiful thing. It also helps you with self-confidence. When you are useful to other humans, when you help them rise, your self-image gets a boost. But we ought to be generous in a wise way, in a mindful way.

Sometimes the way of forgiveness and tolerance is a wise choice because it can make people better. But sometimes it's not, because it just makes people comfortable with their own toxicity. In such a case, effective boundaries might be a better lesson. In the world, we need more tolerance of divergent opinions and backgrounds, but less tolerance of toxic behavior.

You may not agree with my differentiation between niceness and goodness. Yet we need a way to differentiate being kind in a wise manner from being kind in a doormat manner, so that feels like a helpful distinction. Here is my question for you, to help you discern between the two: Are you kind because you need to be or because you *want* to be? Is it a habit or a choice? If you never exercise the option of not being kind, then your kindness is likely unbalanced, and there will be shadow sides to it.

What will happen if you are not kind? Observe the answers that bubble up in you. Is it a "Nothing will happen, but people may suffer, and I could have made their life better" type of thing? Or is it "They may get angry at me. There will be confrontation, and I may get rejected"? Is your kindness based on love, or is it based on fear?

If a seemingly generous act is not aligned with your values, don't do it. The act could be complying with a request, letting go of your needs to fulfill another's, or keeping quiet while the person in front of you unloads their emotional garbage. If it's not aligned, don't do it, and embrace the consequences for the relationship, whatever they are. If a requirement for keeping a relationship is that you need to go against your own needs and values from time to time, then why would you want to stay in such a relationship? That wouldn't be kind to yourself, and not helpful to the other person's higher self either.

Don't do something for others if it goes against your values. It's not worth it. You will resent it, and that makes the act of kindness pointless. Then you will have lost on both fronts: the values and the act of kindness. Instead, practice *wise* kindness.

The Bottom Line

Learning how to live inside out in the midst of toxic people and messy human relationships is difficult—but essential. Learn this art little by little by practicing the techniques in this chapter. What types of people does your aspirational identity seek to have in your life? How does your ideal self communicate your needs, wants, and opinions? How does it respond to toxicity and boundaries crossed?

The core message of this chapter is to remember your core values and aspirational identity when interacting with people. Relate from that space, and your relationships will be an affirmation of who you are, rather than something that undermines your self-confidence and self-esteem.

PART 5

MAKING IT ALL WORK

18.

Stay Disciplined

Discipline is choosing between what you want
now and what you want most.

—attributed to Abraham Lincoln

A disciplined mind leads to happiness.
An undisciplined mind leads to suffering.

—Dalai Lama

There are no shortcuts to any place worth going.

—Beverly Sills

Like any other journey of transformation, moving from self-doubt to self-confidence requires self-discipline. There are three reasons for this.

The first reason is that for these techniques to be really effective you need to practice them consistently, even when you may not *feel like* doing them.

The second reason is that you will meet many obstacles in this process. These could be external obstacles, such as an unhelpful environment, toxic people in your life, or busyness; or they could be internal obstacles, such as laziness, lack of motivation, lack of clarity, distractions, procrastination, fears, or excuses. It is only self-discipline that will help you continue on the journey until fruition, despite all the challenges that will make you want to quit.

The third reason is that having self-discipline, in itself, makes you more confident. The more you take consistent action on your goals, live aligned with your values, build positive habits, and accomplish difficult things, the more confident you will feel. As you progress in this journey, you'll not only increase your self-confidence but also develop your self-discipline skills, which can then be used to achieve your other goals.

Self-discipline is not self-punishment, but self-respect. It is you keeping your promises to yourself. It is you prioritizing the most important things in your life and living in alignment with your values day after day. Doing so is important both in external goals (such as career, health, and finances) as well as more internal goals (such as embodying your aspirational identity).

Many people think of self-discipline as something that's restricting and painful. This is mostly because the way this topic is being taught these days overemphasizes willpower and mental toughness. It's more of a "bulldozer approach" to goals and habits, so I call it the *military* self-discipline. On the other hand, I teach it as awareness *first*, then willpower. This way is gentler, more sustainable, and more universal. I call this approach Mindful Self-Discipline, and if you're interested in learning more, I refer you to my book of the same name, which goes into detail on all the tools behind this framework. When you are in touch with your deepest aspirations and understand the true nature of self-discipline, you will see that self-discipline is here to serve you, that it is your biggest ally.

Throughout this book we have covered some of the tools and principles of Mindful Self-Discipline, such as the POWER Visualization, PAW Method, ROAR Method, and the Not Now technique. Now I'll give you an overview of how you can organize all that you've learned into *daily disciplines*, so that you can really get the results you are seeking.

YOUR DAILY DISCIPLINES

There are different ways to implement the Wise Confidence framework. Here I will suggest a general structure you can use to plug in your favorite practices from the book.

Morning Practice

An ideal morning practice includes two things: meditation and daily alignment. These make up the foundation of this work, which is why we dedicate a good amount of time to it. It could take anywhere from fifteen to thirty minutes, depending on your needs and available time.

Throughout this book you've learned many different meditation practices; however, you *don't need* to do them all. In fact, you cannot. Instead, just focus on what will move the needle the most for you, at this phase in your life. I suggest you choose *one* meditation technique and practice it daily for at least twenty-one consecutive days before trying a new one. When you've gotten what you need from a particular practice, then you can move on to another one. (Refer to the *Index of Practices* at the back of the book for a quick reference to all the techniques covered.)

After meditation, complete your Daily Alignment Practice of remembrance, affirmation, and visualization. (Review chapter 8 for details.)

Ongoing Shifting

In your morning practice you are awakening a new way of being, and throughout the day you are putting it into practice. You do so by shifting to your aspirational identity multiple times each day, whenever you notice that you are gravitating toward the conditioned identity. The framework for this shift is the PAW Method (see chapter 8).

You pause your automatic patterns, become aware of your aspirational identity, and if needed, use some willpower to realign to your Power Words or to apply a technique from the book that makes sense in the moment. With this, you are making a shift from the old to the new, from self-doubt to self-confidence.

The step of willpower at the end of PAW is whatever works for you. Here are some examples:

- shifting your mindset by using the *Deconstruct and Replace* technique (ch. 9)

- releasing painful emotions with the *ROAR Method* (ch. 10)

- *witnessing* negative thoughts and letting them pass (ch. 10)

- using the *Not Now technique* to stop engaging with self-doubt (ch. 10)

- remembering your *core strengths* and leaning on them (ch. 5)

- breaking down the challenge ahead of you into *baby steps* (ch. 8)

- releasing *unrealistic expectations* and being kind to yourself (ch. 9)

- using *active imagination* for shifting your state (ch. 11)

- anchoring the state of confidence in your body via the *LION Mudra* (ch. 12)

- shifting your *posture* and body language to embody confidence (ch. 14)

- *speaking* with greater confidence (ch. 14)

- deciding to *act despite fear* and self-doubt (ch. 15)

- setting *boundaries* with a person (ch. 17)

The same advice about meditation also applies here: choose one or two approaches that you feel most attracted to and focus on them for a period of time, until they become second nature. If instead you try a different technique each time, it will be impossible for you to master any of them, and there will always be some confusion around which one to apply in the moment.

Every time you complete the PAW Method and use one of the techniques, you make a deposit in your self-confidence account (+1); every time you forget and gravitate toward self-doubt or negative self-talk, you are getting into self-confidence debt (-1). That choice is within your power, and you exercise it several times a day, every day.

Evening Review[1]

At night, before going to bed, take a couple of minutes to do the GAIA journal. GAIA is an acronym for gratitude, awareness, intention, and alignment. To practice it, simply ask yourself the following:

Gratitude: *When did I show up as my aspirational identity today (+1)?*

Feel grateful about it. Celebrate your wins, however small. This helps reinforce your new way of being.

Awareness: *When did I gravitate to the conditioned identity today (-1)?*

Simply become aware of it, without beating yourself up. You have just realized a point for improvement, an opportunity for growth.

Intention: *What will I do better tomorrow?*

Reaffirm your intention to do better next time and to live from your aspirational identity. It could be something as simple as "I commit to remembering to use PAW at least three times" or "I will push through my comfort zone when communicating my boundaries tomorrow."

Alignment: *How would I rate myself in living my Power Words today?*

Choose one Power Word to focus on each week and rate yourself from one to ten on how well you practiced it today. This trains your brain to keep your Power Words top of mind, and the result is that you align yourself with them more often.

These questions help you learn from your experience and keep you engaged in the journey. Self-reflection is the mother of wisdom. If you are not reflecting on your life experiences, on your nature and behavior, you are not really growing. Regular self-reflection is, thus, an important element of Wise Confidence.

The Daily Disciplines of *Wise Confidence*
Living Inside Out

Daily Alignment / Meditation — Morning

PAW Method + Favorite Technique — All Day

GAIA Journaling — Evening

ORGANIZE YOUR LIFE

I cannot close this book without briefly touching on two other aspects of self-discipline that also boost your confidence: organization and focus. These are big topics that would require a whole book or course to cover properly. Here, my intent is simply to raise awareness of their impact on your confidence.

Organization is the practice of optimizing your physical space, digital space, and routines so you can be more focused, calm, and effective. It allows you to navigate your environment with less friction, thus freeing up your energy and attention. The opposite of organization is *chaos*, which is inefficient, distracting, and exhausting.

When you are disorganized in daily life, you forget things, are late for meetings, don't prepare enough for opportunities, often get distracted, lose sight of important tasks, can't find stuff, drop the ball at work, and take much longer to complete tasks. As a result of all this, your mind is busier, you feel overwhelmed, and you have less energy to face challenges in life.

It is hard to feel confident when you can't keep your life and environment in order. It's also hard to remain confident about your effectiveness when you feel overwhelmed with the number of things you need to do and are not clear on your priorities. We naturally feel that an organized person is more centered, reliable, and capable. We tend to feel the opposite about disorganized people.

Focus is your capacity to concentrate all your mental energy on a single task, activity, or goal. As we saw in chapter 1, focus is a form of power (*manas shakti*). If you regularly allow your mind's power to leak out through distractions, multitasking, and the pursuit of instant gratification, then you will feel less capable—and thus less confident. Focus enhances the determination/willpower element of self-confidence.

There are two major aspects of focus:

- Macro Focus: knowing your core values, aspirations, and priorities, then organizing your life around them. You create empowering structures in your life—such as a morning routine, day planning, and journaling—so you can focus your time and energy on what matters most. Macro focus relates to the Aspiration Pillar.

- Micro Focus: knowing how to tame the monkey mind and keep it concentrated on the task at hand. Micro focus relates to the Awareness Pillar and is the fruit of meditation practice, organization, and tweaking your environment to facilitate focus.

I encourage you to improve your focus and organization skills, in whatever way suits you, to further strengthen your self-confidence. And if you want some support with this, you can check out the *Work With Me* section at the end of the book.

COMMIT TO NEVER ZERO[2]

To truly transform yourself, you need to commit to the journey fully. Motivation may get you started on the path, but it's only self-discipline that will help you see it through to the end. Motivation is the initial spark, while self-discipline is continuously fanning the fire. Don't depend on motivation, which fluctuates; instead, make a strong commitment.

In Mindful Self-Discipline, we call this a *Never Zero commitment*. You make a resolution to follow your chosen habit every day, no matter what, for a certain period of time. For self-confidence, it means that you commit to shifting to your aspirational identity and practicing confidence every day, no matter what, even if just once a day. This could be the commitment to your morning practice (meditation and alignment), or to going beyond your comfort zone every day, or to applying any other technique from this book.

Your commitment to your aspirational identity is lifelong, but the specifics of it could change from time to time. For example, perhaps you start with a Never Zero commitment of doing exposure therapy daily for one hundred days, then after that you might want to commit to using the Not Now technique three times a day for a month, and then move on to something else according to your evolving needs. The underlying purpose of all those commitments, however, is always the same: becoming your aspirational identity.

The main element of the *Never Zero commitment* is that it's uncompromising. You decide on the minimum acceptable version of your practice, then resolve to *never* go to sleep at night without having done it. It doesn't need to be a big commitment of time; in fact, it is better if it is small and easy to follow, so that you can keep at it even on the difficult days. The essential thing is that it be uncompromising.

Uncompromising means that there are NO acceptable excuses. The commitment is non-negotiable; you keep it daily, no matter what. This shows that you are *committed* to this change and not merely interested in it. You are committed to taking a step toward your aspirational identity every day and live your Power Words.

A 100 percent commitment is actually easier than a 99 percent commitment—because it helps you avoid decision fatigue. When the rule is flexible (99 percent), any day could be an exception day, so every day you need to consider if this is the time to build confidence or the time to listen to self-doubt. But when the commitment is uncompromising (100 percent), there is nothing to think about. Your mind is freed from the burden of weighing your options every time. This saves you energy and gives you peace of mind.

Never Zero is almost a *do-or-die* type of commitment. This expression may feel exaggerated, but it is how inner strength is forged. This strength of determination leads to self-respect, self-confidence, and self-love.

With that, you can mold yourself into the person you aspire to be. With that, you can achieve anything.

It may feel scary to make a commitment like this, even for a small change, because it's powerful and unapologetic. Take this fear as a good sign. You are moving out of your comfort zone. You are placing a big bet on yourself. You are holding tight to your vision, to your ideal self. Many good things will come out of it.

19.

Spirituality and
Self-Confidence

Never think there is anything impossible for the soul.

—Swami Vivekananda

*With the realization of one's own potential
and self-confidence in one's ability,
one can build a better world.*

—Dalai Lama

I can do all things in him that strengtheneth me.

—Philippians 4:13

The concepts, techniques, and tools taught in this book so far don't require you to believe in any metaphysical theories or dogmas; they will work regardless of your spiritual, religious, or philosophical point of view. They work for atheists, materialists, agnostics, Christians, Buddhists, pagans, and anyone else—because they are based on how our psyche works and how our body and emotions work. Having said that, many ancient spiritual traditions offer us valuable lessons that can *supercharge* our self-confidence. Here I distill the essence of such lessons as I've internalized them in my decades of study and practice.

If you are open to spirituality, the worldview and beliefs shared in this chapter can add a layer of depth, meaning, and strength to your self-confidence journey. If you are *not* open to spirituality, feel free to skip this chapter. At this point in the book, you have already learned plenty of effective tools for your journey.

What Is Spirituality?[1]

It is challenging to define spirituality in a way that encompasses all its manifestations and makes everyone happy, yet we need a definition so we can be somewhat on the same page. Here is my working concept:

> Spirituality is a worldview and a way of living based on the intuition that there is more to life than what meets the senses, more to the universe than purposeless mechanics, more to consciousness than electrical impulses in the brain, and more to our existence than the physical body and its needs.
>
> Spirituality embraces this mystery and seeks to explore it. It often involves the belief in a higher form of intelligence or Consciousness as the source of the universe, life after death, and the existence of subtler levels of reality. It is an answer to the deep human thirst for meaning, connection, truth, and peace. It incorporates the transcendental aspect of human existence, the depth of our being, and gives context to transcendental experiences.

Spirituality is not the same as religion. Religion is one of the manifestations of spirituality; you can be spiritual but not religious. For the purposes of this chapter, it doesn't matter what form of spirituality you believe or practice, only that you are aware of the nonmaterial aspect of life and have the willingness to explore it.

A SPIRITUALITY OF EMPOWERMENT

Self-confidence does not play the same role in all spiritual traditions. Some forms of spirituality don't put any emphasis on it; others may even actively discourage it, arguing that it's a trap of the ego. I believe they are criticizing the shadow sides of self-confidence (arrogance), not *wise* confidence. If you were to read a biography of the founder of that path, you will find an empowered individual full of courage, determination, integrity, and self-belief—in other words, confidence.

Other spiritual paths put great importance on self-confidence, although some of them may talk about it mostly as the absence of self-doubt, rather than as a quality in and of itself. As a general rule, spiritual paths that emphasize the importance of effort and willpower (e.g., Yoga, Tantrism, and some lineages of Buddhism) will have a positive view of self-confidence, while paths that emphasize surrender, letting go, and determinism (such as some devotional paths and nondual spirituality) tend to scoff at the concept.

One of the problems in our world is that bad people are confident and good people are often not. In many cases, our spirituality is not help-ing the situation. I would love to see spiritual people be more confident, empowered, and successful—which is one of the reasons why I wrote this book. I'd love to see good-hearted men and women be influential, wealthy, and powerful. I'd love to see you, dear reader, wake up and roar!

So if the journey of self-confidence is important to you, it is worth reflecting on whether your approach to spirituality—and your spiritual-ity's approach to life—are supporting your aspirational identity or not. If there is a contradiction of goals between your spirituality and your values, that discrepancy needs to be resolved in one way or another, or else your heart and energy will be divided, and progress will be difficult.

My goal with this chapter is not to convert you to any particular path, criticize any tradition, or promote any dogma, but to make a synthe-sis of spiritual principles across different traditions where they overlap with the theme of self-confidence. In this overview, I have, naturally, leaned more toward the schools of thought that are life-affirming and have a more positive view of personal development. The teachings of my spiritual master (some of which were briefly included in chapter 17) and the many quotes throughout this book from the fiery Swami Vivekananda clearly show my inclination for what I call a "spirituality of empowerment." Let's now dip our toes into some of its core tenets.

FOUR HELPFUL BELIEFS

Here are four things I believe in that have helped take my confidence, peace of mind, and willpower to a whole new level. They are some of the recurring lessons I've learned during more than two decades of spiritual exploration of several traditions.

Belief #1: You Have an Unbreakable Core

Most spiritual traditions teach that the essence of who you are is pure, immaterial, unshakable, and immortal. Call it Soul, Spirit, Self, Consciousness, Buddha Mind, Source, or whatever you like. This essence existed long before your personality was formed—i.e., before your conditioned identity—and will continue to exist after the death of your body.

If you fully adopt this way of seeing and live your life from it, then your self-confidence will have a *transcendental* foundation. You are not confident because of how talented, smart, or successful you are or because of how much you have achieved. You are confident because you are anchored in the infinite possibilities of your spiritual essence. You know that deep down you are like a diamond—shiny, solid, unbreakable, and able to cut through all obstacles. In the philosophy of *living inside out*, your essence is as "in" as it gets. It is the ultimate foundation of self-confidence.

This means that there is something in you that is not broken, was never broken, and can never be broken. Your core is a source of infinite energy, wisdom, and power in the depths of your heart. It is not something you need to create, but something you *discover*, connect with, and merge with. When you are in touch with it, you have a different type of confidence. Not the confidence of the fool, not the overconfidence of arrogance, but *wise* confidence. This confidence is in a layer deeper than the monkey mind, deeper than the inner critic, and deeper than your traumas and shortcomings.

This Source needs to be experienced, not merely understood. Once you *experience* it, you won't need to believe in it, yet you are unlikely to ever experience it if you don't first firmly believe that it's there. Doubt and skepticism cut off access to that Source by keeping you stuck in the realm of the analytical mind.

How do you get in touch with that essence? There are many ways, and the process will greatly vary from person to person. In general, we connect through:

- consistent prayer and meditation practice
- spiritual study and deep reflection
- faith (in the teachings, in a Higher Power, or in the spiritual master)
- plant medicine
- spontaneous experience

Until this becomes a lived experience, it will be something you simply believe in. Perhaps you believe in it intuitively, or as part of your spiritual worldview, or you could just believe in it because it's a great hypothesis—one upon which an empowered life can be built.

Connecting with your transcendental essence enhances your integrity and self-belief—two of the core ingredients of self-confidence. When you realize, deeply, that the same intelligence that has created the cosmos is within you, would you have any reason to doubt yourself?

Belief #2: You Have a Deep Purpose

Many spiritual philosophies emphasize living with a strong sense of purpose. They teach that we are here to grow and contribute our own gifts, perspectives, and uniqueness. There is a sense of duty (*dharma*) toward who we can be and what we can give—a sense of *I must do this*. It's a duty to explore your full potential, be the best version of yourself, then live and serve from that higher ground.

A caterpillar must become a butterfly; the seed of an oak tree must become an oak tree. The impulse of purpose and growth is present in all forms of life. When we honor it, we experience meaning, happiness, and fulfillment; when we ignore it, we don't.

> *If you deliberately plan on being less than you are capable of being,*
> *then I warn you that you'll be unhappy for the rest of your life.*

> —Abraham Maslow

There is an innate sense of purpose planted deep in your heart, and it's pointing the way forward for you. Believe that you have all the skills you need, even if they're only in seed form, to fulfill your life's purpose. Notice how this changes the way you feel. Then continuously affirm that reality by living in alignment with your aspirational identity.

When you fully embrace your purpose, there is this sense that "I *have to* succeed at this. This is my purpose, so it must happen." This is not the "I have to" of "shoulding" yourself, but "I have to" in the sense of inner alignment, in the sense that there is a higher power guaranteeing it shall happen, as long as you show up with all that you are. Just like the caterpillar *has to* break through its cocoon and become a butterfly, you *have to* grow to your full potential.

Being connected with a deeper sense of purpose gives you courage and determination—two of the core ingredients of self-confidence.

Belief #3: Your Life Is Your Training Ground
When Tony Robbins was asked which core belief has been most helpful in his life, he replied, "That life is happening *for* you, not to you." The same message is echoed by many other voices in the personal development world. And it is a *belief,* an act of faith. It is something that cannot be proven true or false, but it is definitely helpful and empowering. If you believe in an intelligent and compassionate universe you may, like Tony Robbins, have the resilience and resourcefulness that comes from knowing that everything happens for your greater benefit.

The most important decision we make is whether we believe
we live in a friendly or hostile universe.

—attributed to Albert Einstein

What happens when you look at life through the lens of "Everything that is happening is for my greater benefit"? Well, you'll begin looking at the silver linings in life. You will not crumble when meeting adversity, but instead you'll have the mindset that adversity is here to polish your soul. You live with the attitude that whatever is on your plate is what needs to be on your plate and that you have the capacity to deal with it—otherwise it wouldn't be there.

This belief that everything in life is a test, an exercise, and an opportunity to grow is a concept that's taught by many spiritual teachers. Adopting it develops the qualities of courage and optimism in you, which are two of the ingredients of Wise Confidence.

Belief #4: Your Mind Matters

The same Source that manifested the cosmos exists inside of you. You are a spark of that fire—it's all one. Knowing that truth, you can choose the spiritual goal of merging back into the Source and disappearing, or you can choose the spiritual goal of coming forth and playing as the Source in manifestation, expressing the infinite potentialities of consciousness. Different spiritual paths will embrace one goal or the other. If you've picked up this book, I can only assume you are more inclined to the latter.

The final principle of the intersection of spirituality and self-confidence is that your mind shapes your reality. Not only in the psychological sense of determining how you interpret things, what you focus on, and how you engage with life, but also in the metaphysical sense of creating things, events, changes, and opportunities in the "subtle world" that eventually get materialized in this world. Yes, your mind *matters*!

The view of spirituality is that consciousness produces matter, not the other way around. The belief that our thoughts and will can affect reality made its way into the world of personal development via the New

Thought Movement in the US and bestselling self-help classics such as James Allen's *As a Man Thinketh*, Napoleon Hill's *Think and Grow Rich*, Neville Goddard's *How to Manifest Your Desires*, and Rhonda Byrne's *The Secret*. The concept of manifestation made its way into our culture and worldview by concealing the spiritual and esoteric aspects of this practice and giving it a psychological angle. As the decades passed, the emphasis on concentration and willpower (present in the original works) disappeared, and we were left with the empty promise that if we just visualize it and believe it, it will happen.

That is not the case.

Many spiritual traditions have taught over the centuries that if you hold on to a thought for long enough, it *has to* materialize. But that doesn't mean that all our thoughts become something. The mind of the average person is busy, distracted, and undisciplined. The power of such a mind is diluted between thousands of different thoughts and desires, some of which even contradict each other. It's quite possible that no thought gets enough energy to make anything happen. The result of this? A sense of frustration and powerlessness.

Compare that with the disciplined person who knows what they want, focuses continuously on the same goals, remembers them daily, and takes consistent action on them with full conviction. Such intentions are much more likely to materialize not only because of the consistent action taken in the physical world but also because of the constant charging of that intention in the subtle world. Concentration and willpower are the missing elements for you to tap into your innate powers.

How much more confident would you feel if you knew, and felt, that there is an infinite potential inside your mind waiting to be expressed?

When covering affirmations in chapter 8, you learned the four ingredients for tapping into the creative power of the mind: concentration, willpower, faith, and feeling. Yet perhaps back then you thought they only had a psychological dimension to them. Now you know they also work on a deeper layer.

Given all this context, you now can realize that confidence is not only about putting yourself in a psychological condition that makes success more likely. It does that, of course. But it also charges your goals with the energy of belief and determination. Confident people are not more successful in life *only* because they take bolder steps, but also because their thoughts and desires are more powerful and magnetic. Their minds *matter* more.

A visual metaphor might come in handy here. To build a simple electromagnet like one you'd make in school, you coil a copper wire around an iron nail and connect each end of the wire to a battery. The polarities of the battery then create the current that travels through the copper wire and magnetizes the nail, which then attracts metallic items nearby.

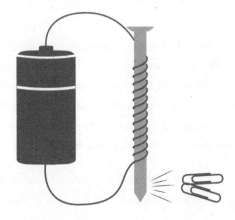

The ancient concept of the mind's power to "manifest"—overly simplified and commercialized by the Law of Attraction movement—works in a similar manner. Your body is the nail, your mind is the battery, and your thought or desire is the copper wire. The stronger are your concentration, willpower, faith, and feeling, the stronger is your battery and the resulting magnetic pull. Then, when you take action toward your goals, that action has a very different quality to it.

It's important to notice, however, that even the slightest doubt or inner resistance in your mind interrupts the flow of the mind energy (*manas shakti*), just like bending the copper wire in the opposite direction completely prevents electromagnetism from being created. This is in line with the idea of integrity being essential to self-confidence and self-doubt being the greatest enemy.

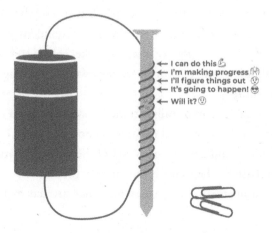

When you believe that your purpose, your will, your intention *must* prevail no matter what, and when you hold fast to that conviction in the face of every challenge, then it *will* prevail. But know that science will not, currently, help you get to this conclusion. Understanding this will require either spiritual insight or faith. And then you can put it to practice, wholeheartedly, and see what results happen for you.

> *The high road to success is to act as if*
> *it were impossible to fail, and it shall be.*
>
> —Unknown

Have full trust that when you give your best and stay true to your values, all will eventually be all right and turn out for your greatest benefit—even if in a different way than expected. Such an act of faith will give you great confidence and peace of mind throughout all of life's challenges.

Believe that success is inevitable. This doesn't mean that you can get lazy about it, skip preparation, and not take massive action. That is *not* Wise Confidence. What it means is that all your efforts, focus, preparation, and inner work happen within the larger space of absolute conviction that you will succeed.

Believe that you *are* your aspirational identity. Treat that belief as a reality, and act from that point of view. In other words, have confidence about your confidence. Stop telling yourself that you are not confident because of this and that. With all the tools you have learned in this book, self-confidence is something you can choose, moment after moment.

If you believe that you partake of the same essence as the Source, then you can engage in the same divine activity—you can create. You cannot create a universe of cosmic proportions, of course, but you can be the creator of your *own* universe.

Living inside out is about us being the creators of ourselves, the gods of our own universe. It is complete self-mastery. That, I believe, is what it means to be ultimately aligned with our spiritual essence and purpose.

20.

Three Final Keys

Arise, awake and do not stop until the goal is reached.
True progress is slow but sure.

—Swami Vivekananda

I have learned that success is to be measured
not so much by the position one has reached in life
as by the obstacles he has overcome while trying to succeed.

—Booker T. Washington

Energy and persistence conquer all things.

—Benjamin Franklin

Wise Confidence is a balanced approach to developing self-confidence, a way of developing this important virtue without falling into the shadows of arrogance, conceit, delusion, or selfishness. You learned the framework of the three pillars of self-confidence—Aspiration, Awareness, Action—and the central concept of *living inside out.*

- Aspiration is your north, your map for living inside out.

- Awareness gives you the tools to shift away from the conditioned self.

- Action is acting, relating, and living from your aspirational self.

You now have all you need to show up in your life with more confidence, deal with self-doubt, and shift your identity, so that your transformation becomes permanent. Most of the tools you have learned in this book are also useful in any other journey of self-transformation—such as from anxiety to calmness, anger to compassion, or depression to joy.

So, what do you do next? For your transformation to be permanent, you need to become a sincere practitioner of Wise Confidence. Do the exercises and implement what you've learned into daily disciplines. Use the structure suggested in chapter 18 to make these practices part of your daily life. I also strongly recommend that you create a recurring calendar event to review your notes from this book once a month and integrate more of its principles. This is essential for you to dive deep and unpack the many layers of meaning behind each idea and truly implement this system.

THE THREE VIRTUES

Personal growth and healing are a little bit like slowly chipping away at a wall—the wall that separates who you are today from who you want to be (your aspirational identity). You don't know how thick the wall is. You don't know how close to success you are. All you can do is to continue chipping away, day after day, with the best tools at your disposal. You have a clear goal (to break down the wall), but you are fully focused on the *process*, rather than obsessing about how long it will take.

In practical terms, this means that, to make all of this work, you need to cultivate three key virtues: patience, perseverance, and determination.

Patience

When you have *patience*, you are committed to the journey for the long-term. You can stay on the path even when the progress is slower than you expected. You don't fall into the trap of false hope syndrome, which is believing that the results will come quickly and effortlessly—an idea widely exploited by greedy marketers who want to sell you "overnight success" solutions.

Be patient with all the times you apply the techniques and don't get immediate results—if you succeed one out of every ten attempts, it's not a bad start! Be patient with the times when you make some progress and then lose that progress. Be patient with the fact that sometimes you'll need to return to the basics, and try baby steps again. Be patient with the times when nothing seems to work and you find yourself getting confused and losing hope.

Feelings of low self-esteem will show up from time to time, as will self-doubt. All of this is due to the past momentum of your conditioned identity, and it's part of the process. They are temporary, so don't get worried about them. Don't get disheartened. Allow yourself to have bad days, and know that they will pass. They don't mean that you are a failure or that the process is not working.

Patience means that this transformation is important enough that it's worth the wait. Sure, we focus on the best tools available, so that the path can be as smooth as possible. But it is still a process and will take time. Patience means releasing that sense of hurry and playing the long game—but without getting lazy about the effort that you need to put in today.

Perseverance

When you have perseverance, you get up every time you fall. You can do that when you have clarity of purpose—meaning that you know how important this self-transformation is for you and you are committed to expressing your full potential. When you are aware of the type of life you can live when you are grounded in Wise Confidence and you know the pains of living in self-doubt, persevering on the path becomes much easier.

Perseverance requires a growth mindset—that is, the belief that growth is possible for you, that *change* is possible. It is knowing that whatever skill, mindset, knowledge, or quality you may lack, you can develop. It is deciding that you are not a quitter and that you haven't come this far just to turn back.

When you meet adversity in your path, welcome it with open arms. Know that it is life polishing the diamond of your soul. Then, charged with this mindset of purpose, continue on your path. Find the next baby step and take it, regardless of what the negative voices in your mind have to say.

This persistence in the face of adversity is a form of courage and openness—it shows that you are not afraid of emotional pain. Rather than giving up upon meeting challenges, you take a deep breath, reconnect to your purpose, and see what is the best way to tackle that challenge.

Patience and perseverance are twin virtues, meaning that they often come together and feed one another. They are important not only for developing self-confidence but also for achieving any other goals you have. When you know you have the strengths of patience and perseverance, you naturally feel more confident, because you know that if you fully commit to something, it's just a matter of time until you achieve it. On the other hand, lacking patience and perseverance makes you feel less capable.

In summary: if you get up every time you fall, you'll feel confident; if you give up, you'll feel defeated, and that will feed an identity of low self-esteem.

Perseverance also means continuing your practices even after you have made some progress and are already satisfied. I can't tell you how many times I've seen people begin a meditation practice to calm their anxiety and then stop the practice as soon as they experience some relief. When they do, they almost always relapse to old ways of thinking, feeling, and functioning.

There is a saying in coaching, "The reason why you've come is not the reason why you are here." You've likely come to this work, to this book, simply wanting to feel more confident—but you may have found something far deeper. The practices you have learned here will definitely help you fulfill your initial intention, yet they can give you much more.

If you continue on the path and persevere past the initial successes, you will come to understand what that is. You will have gained far more than what you were initially seeking.

Determination

Both patience and perseverance come naturally if you have the quality of *determination*. If you are fully determined, fully committed to getting the fruits of this journey no matter what, then you will naturally persevere through the ups and downs and be patient about the process.

Determination is having a clear vision and a strong commitment to fulfill that vision. It is the willingness to do what it takes because you know it's worth it. It is having a strong resolve (*sankalpa*) and unbreakable will. It is going *never zero*.

When you are determined, you think about your goal day and night. You desire it intensely. That thought-current then gets energized by your constant attention, intention, and emotion. It becomes so strong that it overrides all fears, anxieties, and doubts. All obstacles melt away in the presence of such fire. They have to.

Fill every corner of your mind with determination,
and there will be no place left for self-doubt.

Do whatever you need to do to become self-confident—in a wise manner. Be determined to overcome whatever obstacles come your way. Self-confidence is not a nice-to-have, but a must-have. It is an essential element for you to live a life of greater peace, power, and purpose.

IT'S YOUR TURN

When you have clear goals, believe in yourself, and take self-disciplined action, there is no limit to what you can achieve. When you commit to *living inside out*, nothing can break your self-confidence. And now you know how to do this.

So, what's next? You have a choice. You can think, *Great, I've learned a lot from this book!* then close it and start a new one tomorrow, hoping that somehow just reading these pages was enough for self-confidence to automatically appear in your life.

Or you can *really* take action based on what you have learned, consistently. You can highlight, summarize, review, and seriously think about these concepts. You can create a vision for your aspirational identity and decide to unapologetically live from that vision. You can implement the Daily Alignment Practice, creating a sacred space to check in with yourself. You can live more mindfully so whenever you see yourself gravitating toward the conditioned identity you apply the PAW Method, coupled with your favorite techniques from the book. You can choose to act, speak, and relate based on your designed identity—and do so consistently, in the spirit of Never Zero.

Reading this book can be the beginning of a new life. A big reset. A point of no return. It can be the birth of the new you—the more confident, empowered, and wiser *you*. May this book be the turning point you need to grow into the mighty being you were born to be.

Decide who you want to be. Live *inside out* from that vision. Let go of everything else.

GOING DEEPER

First of all, here is where you can go to download the free resources and meditations that I mentioned throughout the book: MindfulSelfDiscipline.com/wise-confidence-bonuses.

In this book I've shared several principles and exercises you can apply to live with more self-confidence. I have not held anything back. This is the *complete system* of Wise Confidence. If you feel that you have gotten all you need and that you can implement all of this on your own, then I am happy for you and wish you success! You can then skip this section.

On the other hand, you might feel that you want to go deeper, consolidate what you've learned, or get some support integrating this framework into your daily life. Here are three ways you can do that depending on your level of commitment.

LEVEL 1: EXPAND YOUR KNOWLEDGE

Wise Confidence is based on the core framework of my teaching, Mindful Self-Discipline, and they both share the same three pillars of Aspiration, Awareness, and Action. Living inside out from your aspirational identity is an expression of internal self-discipline, and being disciplined, in itself, naturally creates more confidence.

So, the next logical step in your journey could be the *Mindful Self-Discipline* book/audiobook. It teaches you how to deal with obstacles, such as distractions, procrastination, excuses, lack of motivation, and poor time management. It also helps you develop positive habits, break negative habits, strengthen your willpower, improve your focus, find your core values, and cultivate perseverance.

As a companion to *Mindful Self-Discipline*, you can get the wristbands, which have the words *Never Zero* or *Pause Awareness Willpower*. They serve as a constant reminder, an anchor, for you to shift from the conditioned identity to your aspirational identity.

You can learn more about both at MindfulSelfDiscipline.com.

LEVEL 2: CONSOLIDATE YOUR PRACTICE

To take the practice one step further, there is the Mindful Self-Discipline app, which helps you take what you've learned to the next level and *actually* implement the framework of both books, so you can achieve the transformation you seek.

Think of this app as an ongoing training program for self-confidence and self-discipline. Its goal is to help you live a life of greater focus, purpose, and empowerment. It includes:

- exclusive guided meditations

- breathing exercises

- video courses

- step-by-step PAW Method

- a reward engine that keeps you motivated

- the GAIA journal

- reminders for meditation, PAW, and journaling

- members-only Q&As with me

You can learn more about it at MindfulSelfDiscipline.com/app.

LEVEL 3: ACCELERATE YOUR TRANSFORMATION

There is a level of transformation and support that can never happen through a book, however complete. Having the knowledge is one thing; effectively implementing it is something else.

Perhaps you wonder which of the *dozens* of exercises in this book you should focus on and how to go about it. Perhaps you need some support customizing this system for your personality and needs. Perhaps you feel stuck somewhere and know that having some mentorship will help you move forward quicker, saving you the time and pain that comes from the trial-and-error approach. Perhaps you are playing small, held back by certain limiting beliefs and fears. Finally, there may be an inner block you just cannot figure out—a part of yourself that is sabotaging the journey—and you need help resolving it.

You can have the best set of videos for exercising at home or for improving your public-speaking skills, but nothing can compare to having a personal trainer or a one-on-one speaking coach. They will take you to the next level. They will hold you accountable every step of the way and inspire you to be better. They will give you personalized feedback and tips tailored to your needs. They will show you shortcuts that can only be shared face-to-face. You will be much more committed to the process, and thus much more likely to succeed. You will have clarity about what to do and the confidence of knowing you are on the right path. In a nutshell: you will be guided and supported.

The same thing is true for becoming self-confident. So here is my invitation for you: if you want to accelerate your journey toward your aspirational identity and you are willing to invest in yourself, then contact me for coaching at MindfulSelfDiscipline.com/coaching.

Appendix 1: The Yoga of Confidence

I n chapter 12, we mentioned that there are several somatic approaches for clearing emotional blockages and raising your energy levels. This appendix explores key practices from the Yoga tradition that are directly connected to the *manipura chakra*, the energy center located in the solar plexus.

The solar plexus is essential for generating more energy, willpower, and inner fire. It's also important for maintaining good health. In the Yoga tradition we activate the solar plexus through special postures, breathing exercises, meditations, and also through the inner work of overcoming limiting emotions that block our energy—such as shame, fear, disgust, jealousy, laziness, and sadness. For an in-depth study of this topic I suggest you read *Manipura Chakra* by Rishi Nityabodhananda, and for a scientific perspective on the "gut brain," see *The Second Brain* by Michael Gershon.

There are many Yoga postures (*asanas*) that stimulate the solar plexus. Some do so by engaging your core and constantly massaging the plexus, such as exercises that involve continuous leg lifts or leg rotations, as well as the Sun Salutation. Others affect the manipura more deeply by either expanding or squeezing it in one direction and holding that posture for some time. To experiment with this approach, I suggest you try the following postures, ordered from easy to hard: Crocodile Pose (*Makarasana*), Shoulder Pose *(Kandharasana)*, Boat Pose *(Naukasana)*, Bow Pose *(Danurasana)*, and Wheel Pose (*Chakrasana*).

Now let me introduce you to two of my favorite Yoga breathing exercises for the solar plexus: Fire Cleansing and Bellows Breath.

FIRE CLEANSING (AGNISARA)

This practice is one of my favorite Yoga techniques. Practicing it effectively can initially be challenging for most people, as it requires a great level of control over the abdominal muscles. So remember to cultivate patience and perseverance. The Panting Breath practice is a good preparation for this one.

1. Sit on your knees or in a meditation posture, with your spine erect.

2. Inhale deeply, then exhale slowly while fully emptying your lungs.

3. Then hold your breath. Place your open hands on your knees, palms down, straighten your elbows, and lean forward slightly. Bend your neck so your chin touches your chest.

4. In this position, rapidly contract and expand the abdominal muscles while still holding your breath, for as long as you comfortably can. Start with ten movements, and over the months of practice, increase it up to one hundred.

5. When you are done, lift your head up, unlock your arms, move your body back to the original position, then inhale slowly.

6. Take a couple of slow, deep breaths.

7. This completes one round. Practice three rounds like this.

For a more advanced version of this practice, at the end of the round, take one deep breath in and out, then retain the breath and keep empty for as long as possible while holding what is known as the "triple lock" or "great lock" (*mahabandha*) in Yoga. To learn more about this variation, refer to *Asana Pranayama Mudra Bandha* by Swami Satyananda.

BELLOWS BREATH (BHASTRIKA)

Together with *agnisara*, this is the main practice to awaken the *manipura*.

1. Sit on your knees or in a meditation posture, with your spine erect.

2. Inhale deeply, then exhale slowly, one to three times.

3. Now forcefully inhale and exhale through the nose in a quick succession of short breaths. Both inhalation and exhalation should have the same length. When breathing out, the abdominal muscles fully contract (move inward); when breathing in, they fully expand (move outward). Do this for ten to fifty breaths.

4. After the last short exhalation, inhale deeply and slowly, hold your breath for as long as comfortable, then breathe out deeply and slowly.

5. This concludes one round. Take a few normal breaths before going to the next round. Practice three to ten rounds in total.

The rhythm of the short breaths can be one full breath every two seconds, every one second, or even every half a second. But don't worry about increasing the speed of breaths, as this can lead to poor form. It will happen naturally over time. Instead, to deepen the practice, gradually increase the number of breaths per round, while keeping a steady rhythm.

The rather conservative advice of modern Yoga books is to increase each round up to fifty breaths. In my experience, with care and consistent practice, many people can go far beyond that point. Personally, I do rounds of three hundred to twelve hundred breaths, but this came only after several months of daily practice. Caution *must* be exercised, as this can be a rather intense practice.

GENERAL GUIDELINES

Please note that all these practices also have the effect of producing heat in your body and stimulating digestion and blood flow. They are typically not recommended for pregnant women or for people suffering from high blood pressure, inflammatory disorders, or diarrhea. Discontinue the practice if you experience adverse effects, or seek a qualified Yoga teacher. Consult your doctor about the suitability of these practices for you.

The best time to practice these techniques is early in the morning, after going to the bathroom and before breakfast. Do these techniques before your meditation practice, as that will help deepen their effects. In terms of length of time, you can do them for five minutes or up to half an hour over time—it depends on your available time and your goals.

For additional support and guided practices, check out the "Going Deeper" section in this book. Alternatively, seek the guidance of competent Yoga teachers who live what they preach and ideally are themselves full of willpower, energy, and confidence.

Appendix 2: Index of Practices

This book contains a total of sixty-one exercises/techniques. Use this section as a quick practical reference and to mark which ones to focus on. Please remember, you cannot and should not attempt to practice them all; focusing on two or three of them will suffice. That will keep your efforts and energy more focused. After some consistent practice, when the chosen techniques become second nature, you can then add new ones.

In these tables, the type of practice is somewhat of an arbitrary categorization. The "Frequency" column indicates if you only need to practice that particular technique *once*, if you need to practice it for *some time* (as the need arises), or if it should be done *regularly*. The "When" column indicates whether that practice is to be done "in the moment," at a separate time (such as in your morning or evening routine), or both.

Ch	Technique / Exercise	Type	Frequency	When
2	Self-Confidence Audit	Self-Reflection	Once	Separate time
5	Lean on Your Strengths	Other	Regularly	In the moment
5	Find Your Strengths	Self-Reflection	Once	Separate time
5	Strengths Use	Self-Reflection	Once	Separate time

Ch	Technique / Exercise	Type	Frequency	When
5	Weaknesses Self-Awareness	Self-Reflection	Once	Separate time
5	Strengths Journaling	Self-Reflection	Regularly	Separate time
5	Imprinting Confidence	Meditation	Some Time	Separate time
5	Empowered Experiences	Self-Reflection	Once	Separate time
6	Choose Your Symbols	Self-Reflection	Once	Separate time
6	Aspirational Power Words	Self-Reflection	Once	Separate time
6	Choose Your Way of Life	Self-Reflection	Once	Separate time
6	Yoga Nidra for Sankalpa	Meditation	Regularly	Separate time
7	Transition Ritual	Other	Once	Separate time
7	Facing the Worst	Self-Reflection	Once	Separate time
7	Ownership	Mindset	Regularly	In the moment
7	Black and White Clarity	Self-Reflection	Once	Separate time
8	Daily Alignment Practice	Inner Shifting	Regularly	Separate time
8	Baby Steps	Other	Regularly	Both
8	PAW Method / Living Inside Out	Inner Shifting	Regularly	In the moment
8	SMART Goals	Other	Regularly	Separate time

Ch	Technique / Exercise	Type	Frequency	When
9	Failure Mindsets	Mindset	Regularly	Both
9	Cultivate Positive Mindsets	Mindset	Regularly	Both
9	Negative Self-Talk Inventory	Self-Reflection	Once	Separate time
9	Deconstruct and Replace	Mindset	Regularly	Both
10	Witnessing & Labeling	Inner Shifting	Regularly	Both
10	Not Now Technique	Inner Shifting	Regularly	In the moment
10	ROAR Method	Inner Shifting	Regularly	Both
11	Removing Obstacles to Confidence	Inner Shifting	Regularly	Both
11	Dissolving Negative Thoughts	Inner Shifting	Regularly	Both
11	Imagining Confidence	Meditation	Regularly	Both
11	POWER Visualization	Meditation	Regularly	Separate time
11	Meeting Your Future Self	Meditation	Some Time	Separate time
11	Shifting Your Past	Meditation	Some Time	Separate time
12	Piercing the Sun Breathing	Meditation	Regularly	Separate time
12	Fire Cleansing (agnisara)	Meditation	Regularly	Separate time

Ch	Technique / Exercise	Type	Frequency	When
12	Bellows Breath (bhastrika)	Meditation	Regularly	Separate time
12	Inverted Asanas	Other	Regularly	Separate time
12	Panting Breath	Meditation	Some Time	Separate time
12	Awaken Confidence in Your Body	Inner Shifting	Regularly	Both
13	Trataka	Meditation	Regularly	Separate time
13	Loving-Kindness	Meditation	Regularly	Separate time
13	Mantra Meditation	Meditation	Regularly	Separate time
13	Box Breathing	Meditation	Regularly	Separate time
13	Perspective Meditation	Meditation	Some Time	Separate time
14	Power Poses (standing and moving)	Other	Regularly	In the moment
14	Your Voice, Your Power	Other	Regularly	In the moment
14	Look Confident	Other	Regularly	Separate time
14	Throat Chakra Practices	Meditation	Some Time	Separate time
15	Exposure Therapy	Other	Regularly	In the moment
16	Improve Continuously	Other	Regularly	Separate time
17	Setting Boundaries	Other	Regularly	In the moment

Ch	Technique / Exercise	Type	Frequency	When
17	Influencers Detox	Other	Once	Separate time
17	Fire Toxic People	Other	Once	Separate time
18	Organization	Other	Regularly	Both
18	Focus	Other	Regularly	Both
18	Never Zero	Other	Regularly	Both
18	Evening Review	Self-Reflection	Regularly	Separate time
19	Four Helpful Beliefs (optional)	Mindset	Regularly	Both
20	Patience	Mindset	Regularly	Both
20	Perseverance	Mindset	Regularly	Both
20	Determination	Mindset	Regularly	Both

Acknowledgments

Special thanks and acknowledgments:

To my wife, Sepide Tajima, for all the support throughout this journey—from her insightful feedback on the early drafts to taking great care of our little one so I could focus on this project for months.

To the several readers, meditation students, and coaching clients who gave me feedback on the ideas, exercises, and designs of this book.

To everyone who ever attempted to break my spirit, for giving me the opportunities to test my hypothesis and develop unbreakable confidence.

To all the yogis and sages who showed me the path to inner strength without arrogance.

To my spiritual master, whose name I will keep private, for always boosting my confidence and guiding me in the path of wisdom, virtue, and inner power.

Notes and References

CHAPTER 2

1. Daniel Campbell-Meiklejohn, Arndis Simonsen, Chris D. Frith, and Nathaniel D. Daw, "Independent Neural Computation of Value from Other People's Confidence," *Journal of Neuroscience* 37, no. 3 (January 18, 2017): 673–684, jneurosci.org/content /37/3/673.

2. Abdurachman and Netty Herawati, "The Role of Psychological Well-Being in Boosting Immune Response," *African Journal of Infectious Diseases* 12 (2018): 54–61, ncbi.nlm.nih.gov /pmc/articles/PMC5876785/; and Md. Abdul Hannan, Md. Nabiul Islam, and Md Jamal Uddin, "Self-Confidence as an Immune Modifying Psychotherapeutic Intervention for COVID-19 Patients and Understanding of its Connection to CNS-Endocrine-Immune Axis" *Journal of Advanced Biotechnology and Experimental Therapeutics* 3, no. 4 (December 2020): 14–17, ejmanager.com/mnstemps/178/178-1592221000.pdf?t =1676497923.

CHAPTER 7

1. Part of this section was adapted from *Mindful Self-Discipline*.

CHAPTER 8

1. Part of this section was adapted from *Mindful Self-Discipline*.
2. Part of this section was adapted from *Mindful Self-Discipline*.

CHAPTER 10

1. Willoughby B. Britton et al., "From Self-Esteem to Selflessness," *Frontiers in Psychology* 12 (November 2021), doi.org/10.3389 /fpsyg.2021.730972.
2. Part of this section was adapted from *Mindful Self-Discipline*.
3. Part of this section was adapted from *Mindful Self-Discipline*.

CHAPTER 11

1. Naomi I. Eisenberger, Matthew D Lieberman, and Kipling D. Williams, "Does Rejection Hurt? An FMRI Study of Social Exclusion," *Science* 302 (October 10, 2003): 290–292, science .org/doi/10.1126/science.1089134.
2. Ruth A. Lanius, Eric Vermetten, and Clare Pain, *The Impact of Early Life Trauma on Health and Disease: The Hidden Epidemic* (Cambridge: Cambridge University Press, 2010).
3. Daniel L. Schacter and Scott D. Slotnick, "The Cognitive Neuroscience of Memory Distortion," *Neuron* 44, no. 1 (September 30, 2004): 149–160, doi.org/10.1016/j.neuron.2004.08.017; and Brian D. Gonsalves et al., "Memory Strength and Repetition Suppression," *Neuron* 47, no. 5 (September 1, 2005): 751–761, doi.org/10.1016/j.neuron.2005.07.013.
4. Serge Stoleru et al., "Neuroanatomical Correlates of Visually Evoked Sexual Arousal in Human Males," *Archives of Sexual Behavior* 28 (February 1999): 1–21, link.springer.com/article /10.1023/A:1018733420467; and Amy H. Mezulis et al., "Is There a Universal Positivity Bias in Attributions? A Meta-Analytic Review of Individual, Developmental, and Cultural Differences in the Self-Serving Attributional Bias," *Psychological Bulletin* 130, no. 5 (2004): 711–747, doi.org/10.1037/0033 -2909.130.5.711.
5. Ted J Kaptchuk et al., "Components of Placebo Effect: Randomised Controlled Trial in Patients with Irritable Bowel Syndrome," *The BMJ* 336 (May 1, 2008), doi.org/10.1136 /bmj.39524.439618.25; and Arthur J. Barsky, MD et al.,

"Nonspecific Medication Side Effects and the Nocebo Phe-
nomenon," *JAMA* 287, no. 5 (February 6, 2002): 622–627,
jamanetwork.com/journals/jama/article-abstract/194619.

6. Dan Gilbert, "The Surprising Science of Happiness," TED
   Talk at ted.com/talks/dan_gilbert_the_surprising_science_of
   _happiness?language=en.

7. Carey K. Morewedge, Young Eun Huh, and Joachim Vosgerau,
   "Thought for Food: Imagined Consumption Reduces Actual
   Consumption," *Science* 330, no. 6010 (December 10, 2010):
   1530–1533, science.org/doi/10.1126/science.1195701#con1;
   and Esther K. Papies, Wolfgang Stroebe, and Henk Aarts, "The
   Allure of Forbidden Food: On the Role of Attention in Self-
   Regulation," *Journal of Experimental Social Psychology* 44, no.
   5 (September 2008): 1283–1292, sciencedirect.com/science
   /article/abs/pii/S0022103108000747; and Eva Kemps and
   Marika Tiggemann, "A Role for Mental Imagery in the Experience and Reduction of Food Cravings," *Frontiers in Psychiatry* 5
   (2014), ncbi.nlm.nih.gov/pmc/articles/PMC4284995/.

8. In this study, the researchers conducted several experiments
   to investigate the effect of positive fantasies about idealized
   futures on motivation for goal pursuit. They found that when
   participants were asked to imagine that they had already
   achieved their goals, they became less motivated to pursue those
   goals in reality. Source: Heather Barry Kappes and Gabriele
   Oettingen, "Positive Fantasies about Idealized Futures Sap
   Energy," *Journal of Experimental Social Psychology* 47, no. 4
   (July 2011): 719–729, sciencedirect.com/science/article/abs/pii
   /S002210311100031X.

9. Dwight W. Kearns and Jane Crossman, "Effects of a Cognitive
   Intervention Package on the Free-Throw Performance of Varsity
   Basketball Players during Practice and Competition," *Perceptual
   and Motor Skills* 75, no. 3 (December 1992), journals.sagepub
   .com/doi/10.2466/pms.1992.75.3f.1243.

CHAPTER 13

1. Part of this section was adapted from *Mindful Self-Discipline.*
2. Part of this section was adapted from *Mindful Self-Discipline.*

CHAPTER 14

1. Dana R. Carney, Amy J.C. Cuddy, and Andy J. Yap, "Power Posing: Brief Nonverbal Displays Affect Neuroendocrine Levels and Risk Tolerance," *Psychological Science* 21, no. 10 (October 2010), journals.sagepub.com/doi/10.1177/0956797610383437.

CHAPTER 17

1. Part of this section was adapted from *Mindful Self-Discipline.*
2. Igor Pantic, MD, PhD, "Online Social Networking and Mental Health," *Cyber Psychology, Behavior and Social Networking* 17, no. 10 (October 1, 2014): 652–657, ncbi.nlm.nih.gov/pmc/articles/PMC4183915/.

CHAPTER 18

1. Part of this section was adapted from *Mindful Self-Discipline.*
2. Part of this section was adapted from *Mindful Self-Discipline.*

CHAPTER 19

1. Part of this section was adapted from *Mindful Self-Discipline.*

About the Author

Giovanni Dienstmann is a meditation teacher, self-discipline coach, and author who focuses on the intersection between wisdom, peace, and personal empowerment.

As a self-discipline coach, Giovanni has helped hedge fund managers, executives, entrepreneurs, artists, and pro athletes live a more focused and disciplined life. Since 2014 he has coached people to overcome their distractions, procrastination, self-doubt, fear, anxiety, and limiting beliefs.

As a meditation teacher, Giovanni runs one of the most visited meditation blogs on the web. His first book, *Practical Meditation*, is available in eight languages and has popularly been called "the meditation Bible." Giovanni has over twelve thousand hours of personal meditation practice and is a sought-after consultant for award-winning meditation apps. His meditation programs have helped over twenty thousand people start a daily meditation practice, improve their psychological well-being, and master their minds.

Learn more at MindfulSelfDiscipline.com and LiveAndDare.com.

About Sounds True

S ounds True was founded in 1985 by Tami Simon with a clear mission: to disseminate spiritual wisdom. Since starting out as a project with one woman and her tape recorder, we have grown into a multimedia publishing company with a catalog of more than 3,000 titles by some of the leading teachers and visionaries of our time, and an ever-expanding family of beloved customers from across the world.

In more than three decades of evolution, Sounds True has maintained our focus on our overriding purpose and mission: to wake up the world. We offer books, audio programs, online learning experiences, and in-person events to support your personal growth and awakening, and to unlock our greatest human capacities to love and serve.

At SoundsTrue.com you'll find a wealth of resources to enrich your journey, including our weekly *Insights at the Edge* podcast, free downloads, and information about our nonprofit Sounds True Foundation, where we strive to remove financial barriers to the materials we publish through scholarships and donations worldwide.

To learn more, please visit SoundsTrue.com/freegifts or call us toll-free at 800.333.9185.

Together, we can wake up the world.

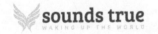

sounds true

WAKING UP THE WORLD